Theories of Language

Theories of Language

— Oriental and Occidental —

Korada Subrahmanyam

D.K. Printworld (P) Ltd.
New Delhi

Cataloging in Publication Data — DK
[Courtesy: D.K. Agencies (P) Ltd. <docinfo@dkagencies.com>]

Subrahmanyam, Korada, 1954–
Theories of language : oriental and occidental / Korada Subrahmanyam.
p. 23 cm.
Includes bibliographical references (p.)
Includes index.
ISBN 13: 9788124604557
ISBN 10: 812460455X

1. Language and languages — Origin. 2. Grammar, Comparative and general. 3. Sanskrit language — Grammar. 4. Sanskrit philology. I. Title.

DDC 415 22

ISBN 13: 978-81-246-0455-7
ISBN 10: 81-246-0455-X
First published in India in 2008

Published and printed by:
D.K. Printworld (P) Ltd.
Regd. Office: 'Sri Kunj', F-52, Bali Nagar
Ramesh Nagar Metro Station
New Delhi-110 015
Phones: (011) 2545 3975; 2546 6019; *Fax*: (011) 2546 5926
E-mail: dkprintworld@vsnl.net
Website: www.dkprintworld.com

Preface

IT had been my dream to make available the theories of language of both Oriental and Occidental origin in a nutshell for the benefit of the students of language science in general. As is obvious, no such work is available although we come across a number of books dealing with the theories separately; the reason being that neither the Oriental scholars nor the Western linguists are thorough in both the streams. However, it is difficult to find a scholar who digested all the systems of Indian philosophy whereas most of the Western scholars try to understand Pāṇini only. As was suggested by Bhartṛhari in *Vākyapadīyam*, one should get acquainted with different Śāstras and Darśanas in order to make one's intellect flavoured with wisdom; and also one cannot decide by simply following his own logic (*prajñā vivekam labhate bhinnairāgamadarśanaiḥ, kiyadvā śākyamunnetum svatarkamanudhāvatā*? 2-484). It is also my long-cherished desire that the treasure of knowledge that is there in different schools and systems of Indian philosophy be made available to the people of the West in general and serious students of linguistics in particular.

Having been born in an orthodox brāhmaṇa family on the banks of the holy river Godāvarī (in the area called Konasīmā), through regular recitation of (*Kṛṣṇa*) *Yajurveda* and study and teaching of different systems I still strive to keep the Oriental thinking green in my mind. I committed *Amarakośa* to my heart at the age of five and underwent training in different *gurukula*s besides the one I had under my father (Late Subrahmanyam), who was a *ghanapāṭhī* and scholar in Pāṇini. My forefathers had tried their best to keep the traditions and customs of Āryas intact through uninterrupted *guru-śiṣya paramparā* (the chain of teacher and desciple). I too had shouldered the responsibility of maintaining the same tradition, of course, in a different manner.

Language had been subjected to micro-analysis and macro-analysis, both at syntactic and semantic levels, right from *varṇa* (phoneme) through *mahāvākya* (discourse) by Indian intelligentsia, thousands of years ago. Almost all the systems and schools of Indian philosophy, including Vyākaraṇa, had discussed the concept of *śabda*. The term *śabda* (*vāk*) is untranslatable. It is used to denote many things, i.e. *varṇa* (phoneme), *prakṛti/pratyaya* (morpheme), *pada* (word), *vākya* (sentence), *avāntara-vākya* (sub-sentence), *mahāvākya* (discourse), the *śabda-pramāṇa, parā, paśyantī, madhyamā, vaikharī* and the ordinary sound. *Ṛk, Yajus, Sāma,* etc. are synonyms of *vākya.*

Among various systems of Indian philosophy, Vyākaraṇa, Pūrva-Mīmāṁsā and Nyāya are considered to be essential for the complete understanding of the concept of *śabda* and its different forms. They are called Padaśāstra, Vākyaśāstra and Pramāṇaśāstra, respectively. A scholar who has got the knowledge of all these Śāstras is called *pada-vākya-pramāṇajña.*

It may be noted that all these systems discussed, in detail, the concept of *śabda* at all the levels. Rather, they are styled so depending on the factor they discussed chiefly. The other systems like Sāṁkhya, Yoga and Uttara-Mīmāṁsā had also expounded the theories of language. But more or less, those are the ones propounded in the said three, i.e. Pada-vākya-pramāṇa-Śāstras.

An attempt is here being made to give a panorama of the theories of language, both ancient and modern. Such an attempt has been necessitated after my observation of two decades of the deplorable scene of the study of language and its theories by scholars across the globe in general and the Indian subcontinent in particular.

On the one side, as it is in the case of other social sciences, most of the linguists in India have been taking up the theories that were postulated in the West (often in Western hemisphere) and working on them. As is obvious, many theories were propounded by the scholars in the West and later they were refuted by the founders themselves. As a result, slowly Indian (and some Western) scholars have realized that one can no longer depend on the modern linguists for a viable and standard theory. Gradually they started tilting towards ancient Indian theories of language. Meanwhile, during the last several years or so, application of electronics has gained momentum and linguists and computer scientists have started trying various languages in computers for machine translation. Most of them have started a serious study of ancient Indian theories of language as they felt that Sanskrit, a natural language supported by Pāṇinian framework only fits the computers.

It is also conspicuous that each and every unit in ancient linguistic science is defined clearly and unambiguously. No definition/rule/norm is revised. There are impeccable solutions to all the problems, both at syntactic and semantic levels.

On the other hand, the scholars of modern linguistic science are still searching for a definition of "word." Scholars are divided on the concept of discourse/text/macro sentence. The theories that are proposed were revised time and again. Meanwhile, the libraries are dumped with books/theses/articles, written taking the theories that were later stamped as untenable. The situation still continues. It is against such a background that a good number of modern linguists started learning the ancient theories. Some of them did a complete volte-face in this regard.

Hyderabad
March 22, 2008

Korada Subrahmanyam
<Korada11@gmail.com>

Contents

Key to Transliteration

VOWELS

अ *a*	आ *ā*	इ *i*	ई *ī*	उ *u*	ऊ *ū*	ऋ *ṛ*	ॠ *ṝ*[1]
(Roman)	(palm)	(it)	(police)	(put)	(rule)	(rig)	
ऌ *ḷ*	ॡ *ḹ*[1]	ए *e*	ऐ *ai*	ओ *o*	औ *au*		
(able)		(there)	(aisle)	(no)	(loud)		

CONSONANTS

Guttural	क *ka*	ख *kha*[2]	ग *ga*	घ *gha*[2]	ङ *ṅa*
	(skate)	(blockhead)	(gate)	(ghost)	(sing)
Palatal	च *ca*	छ *cha*[2]	ज *ja*	झ *jha*[2]	ञ *ña*
	(chunk)	(catch him)	(john)	(hedgehog)	(bunch)
Cerebral	ट *ṭa*	ठ *ṭha*[2]	ड *ḍa*	ढ *ḍha*[2]	ण *ṇa*
	(start)	(anthill)	(dart)	(godhead)	(under)
Dental	त *ta*	थ *tha*[2]	द *da*	ध *dha*[2]	न *na*
	(path)	(thunder)	(that)	(this)	(numb)
Labial	प *pa*	फ *pha*[2]	ब *ba*	भ *bha*[2]	म *ma*
	(spin)	(philosophy)	(bin)	(abhor)	(much)
Semi-vowels	य *ya*	र *ra*	ल *la*[3]	व *va*[4]	
	(young)	(drama)	(luck)	(vile)	
Sibilants	श *śa*[5]	ष *ṣa*[5]	स *sa*	ह *ha*	
	(shove)	(bushel)	(so)	(hum)	
Others	क्ष *kṣa*	त्र *tra*	ज्ञ *jña*		
	(*kṣatriya*)	(*triśūla*)	(*jñānī*)		

अं (ं) *ṁ anusvāra* is a nasal off-glide that immediately follows the pronunciation of a vowel as in *saṁskṛti.*

अः *visarga* = *ḥ* consists in abrupt release of breath after a vowel as in *prātaḥ.*

ऽ *Avagraha* shows non-pronunciation, that is, deletion of "a" after "e" or "o" as in *ime 'vasthitāḥ*. In Vedic Sanskrit, it can also show word division.

HINDI LETTERS (extras)

ँ = *m̐*	ं = ṅ	ड़ = *ṛa*	ढ़ = *ṛha*
(*candrabindu*)	(*anusvāra*)		

---

1 Longer form of the preceding vowel.

2 Aspirated forms of the preceding consonants. The compound words given as examples should be pronounced without a syllabic break at the underlined places. "tha" and "pha" should not be pronounced as fricatives.

3 retroflexed and written as "L *la*" in certain phonetic contexts.

4 Pronounced like "w," without aspiration.

5 "śa" is palatal; "ṣa" cerebral or retroflex.

Introduction
Oriental Theories of Language

ŚABDAS in Sanskrit language can be put under two headings — Vaidika and Laukika. There are four Vedas — *Ṛgveda* (21 branches), *Sāmaveda* (1000), *Yajurveda* (100), and *Atharvaveda* (9). The Vedic literature is too vast and only much less number of branches of each Veda are available today. On the other hand, there are six Vedāṅgas (usually to understand the Vedic literature), viz. Śikṣā (Phonetics), Vyākaraṇam (Grammar), Chandas (Prosody), Niruktam (Etymology and Lexicon), Jyotiṣam (Astrology) and Kalpaḥ (Ritualistic data). There are six Darśanas too, which are useful for salvation, viz. Nyāya, Vaiśeṣika, Pūrva-Mīmāṁsā, Uttara-Mīmāṁsā, Sāṁkhya and Yoga. Apart from this, there are Upavedas, Purāṇas, Upapurāṇas, Kāvyas/Nāṭakas and other works. Besides, there is the Sanskrit that was being spoken. All the works related to the above-mentioned fields were in *laukika-Saṁskṛtam*.

Earlier to Pāṇini, there were grammars separately for Vedic *śabda*s called Prātiśākhya and for classical *śabda*s called Vyākaraṇa. It was Pāṇini, considered to be the most genius on earth, who constructed the famous work, viz. *Aṣṭādhyāyī* (consisting of eight chapters), that is useful for both Vedic and classical *śabda*s. The main difference between both the *śabda*s is the *svara* (accent), i.e. *udātta, anudātta, svarita*, etc. which is very much important in Vedic *śabda*s. Meaning would change if the specified *svara* is not employed. In *laukika-śabda*s, there will be *ekaśruti svara* (where no difference of accents like *udātta* is felt). There is also difference in the form (not meaning) of certain words of Vedic and classical literature.

Laukika	Meaning	Vaidika
Gṛhṇāmi	I'm holding	*Gṛbhṇāmi*
Saṁjahāra	killed/withheld	*Saṁjabhāra*
Dadhāra	put on/held	*Dādhāra*
Hanti	killing	*Hanati*
Dugdhe	milking	*Duhre*
Karṇaiḥ	with ears	*Karṇebhiḥ*

One must have a thorough knowledge of such a vast literature to know the form of *śabda*. In Paspaśāhnika (Introduction) of *Mahābhāṣya*, Patañjali narrates a story that Bṛhaspati started teaching the right *śabda*s to Indra. He could not finish the job even after one thousand divine years. This is about *saṁskṛta-śabda*s. This story indirectly suggests (*arthavādaḥ*) how genius Pāṇini was.

In Indian literary theatre there is no separate branch by name "Linguistics," rather Vyākaraṇa itself is referred to as "Linguistics."

In truth, it is not only Pāṇini who deals with language and related matters. Other systems/schools like Mīmāṁsā (both), Nyāya, Vaiśeṣika, Sāṁkhya, Yoga, Nirukta, Śikṣā and works like *Suśruta-Saṁhitā, Caraka-Saṁhitā, Arthaśāstra* of Kauṭilya and *Parāśaropapurāṇa* also discuss different linguistic aspects. Of course, the origin lies in Vedas. But, since Vyākaraṇam speaks of the entire gamut of things related to linguistic analysis, there too, as Pāṇinīya is an exhaustive treatise in this regard, *Pāṇinīyavyākaraṇam* is quoted/referred to in each case.

Flavouring the language with philosophy is a conspicuous phenomenon in Indian linguistics. Sages of the subcontinent firmly believe that there is a strong anthropological/ philosophical connection between the elements of language and that of spiritual sciences. The concept has got twofold-benefit — attaining *dharma* through employing perfect *śabda*s (rather than imperfect ones which would cause *adharma* to accumulate) and in the long run one can have a standardized language. Secondly, helping towards attaining the main goal, i.e. *mokṣa* (salvation) through *dharma* (*dharma, artha, kāma,* and *mokṣa,* the so-called *puruṣārtha*s should be the goal of every human being according to Indian philosophy). On the other hand, since "language changes," there would be many forms/ structures of words and sentences in every language and the question of standardization draws a blank. This would have long-range influence on translation in general and machine translation in particular. Therefore, the form of *śabda,* its meaning and the relation between the two must follow a standard.

Kātyāyana and Patañjali vociferously express this view at the outset of *Mahābhāṣya* — *siddhe śabdārthasambandhe lokato 'rthaprayukte śabdaprayoge śāstreṇa dharmaniyamaḥ* — Vyākaraṇa (grammar) can be written when the *śabda, artha* and their relation follow a standard, and the task of Śāstra is to notify/prescribe that certain form of a *śabda,* which is already used in a particular *artha* by people, if employed, would render *dharma* (implying that the opposite would give *adharma*).

1

Origin and Development of Ancient Theories of Language

THE terminological words used in linguistic analysis are available in Vedic literature. The following is from *Gopatha Brāhmaṇa*[1] — let us ask/analyse *oṁkāra*, what is *dhātu*? What is *prātipadika*? What is *ākhyāta*? What is *liṅgam*? What is *saṁkhyā* ? What is *vibhakti* (case-ending)? What is *pratyaya* (suffix)? What is *svara* (accent), *upasarga* (prefix) and *nipāta* (the prescribed *śabda*)? What is *vikāra* (alteration)? and What is *vikārī* (the thing altered)? How many *mātra*s has it got? How many *varṇa*s has it got? How many *akṣara*s has it got? How many words has it got? What is *saṁyoga*? What is *sthāna* — *nādānupradāna* and *anukaraṇam*? — Therefore, as far as the available literature is concerned, the origin of linguistic science or that of Vyākaraṇa can be traced back to Vedas.

In *Ṛk-Tantra*,[2] it is clearly hinted that Brahmā was the first author of Vyākaraṇa. He handed down the science to

---

1. *oṁkāram pṛcchāmaḥ, ko dhātuḥ? kim prātipadikam? kim nāmākhyātam? kiṁ liṅgam? kā vibhaktiḥ? kaḥ pratyayaḥ? kaḥ svara upasargo nipātaḥ? kiṁ vaiyākaraṇam? ko vikāraḥ? ko vikārī? katimātraḥ? kativarṇaḥ katyakṣaraḥ? katipadaḥ? kaḥ saṁyogaḥ? kiṁ sthānanādānupradānakaraṇam?* — *Gopathabrāhmaṇam*

2. *brahmā bṛhaspataye provāca, bṛhaspatirindrāya, indro bharadvājāya, bharadvāja ṛṣibhyaḥ, ṛṣayo brāhmaṇebhyaḥ* ।
— *Ṛktantravyākaraṇam*

Bṛhaspati, who taught the same to Indra, who in turn gave it to Bharadvāja. The *ṛṣis* got it from the latter and from them it reached brāhmaṇas.

Patañjali picked up five hymns from *Ṛgveda* and commented them in relation to Vyākaraṇa, in Paspaśāhnika, the introductory part of *Mahābhāṣya*.

As has already been mentioned, there were many popular grammarians, like Āpiśali, Kāśyapa, Gārgya, Gālava, Bharadvāja, Śākaṭāyana, Śākalya, Senaka, Sphoṭāyana, etc. earlier to Pāṇini. Some of them might have been his contemporaries.

There are nine Vyākaraṇas in total, of which only a few are available. Each and every founder and propagator of Vyākaraṇa was concerned about the attainment of *dharma*, that is peculiar to the Indian subcontinent. Therefore, they brought even language, that was being spoken, under the purview of *dharma*. Patañjali discusses this aspect in Paspaśāhnika of his *magnum opus*, viz. *Mahābhāṣya* — one can get sexual satisfaction through a duly married wife as well as a concubine. The restriction, to resort to the former rather than the latter by jurisprudence, is for *dharma*. Similarly, one can kill his appetite by eating any sort of food. Rather, one is restricted from eating certain dishes for the sake of *dharma*. It is in the same manner, that sages had ordained to employ perfect *śabda*s, although the purpose of transformation of meaning is served even by using imperfect *śabda*s. So much so that *artha-jñāna* (understanding the meaning) as well as *dharma*, both shall be the goal of Vyākaraṇa.

Obviously, protecting the form of different *śabda*s through Vyākaraṇa is possible only when the *śabda*, *artha* and the relation between them remain constant.[3] Probably this wise decision is helpful to us in claiming that Sanskrit is the only language that fits computers (in parsing, machine translation, etc.).

Further, there was the question as to how to write a Vyākaraṇa? Whether to list only (perfect) *śabda*s or only (imperfect *śabdas*) *apaśabda*s or both. Following *pariśeṣanyāya* (implication) either list will do. Again in terms of brevity it is the list of *śabda*s rather than *apaśabda*s that is desired. Each *śabda* would have innumerable *apaśabdas* — *gauḥ* is the (perfect) *śabda* — *gāvī, goṇī, gotā, gopotalikā*, etc. *apaśabda*s were being used in the same sense. The form may differ from man to man, house to house, village to village, town to town and dialect to dialect. But even this task consumes much longer time — a single span of life is not sufficient simply to know the complete range of (perfect) *śabda*s. Therefore (says Patañjali in Paspaśāhnika), Pāṇini resorted to the pattern of general and exceptional rules (or *utsarga* — *apavāda sūtra*s).

As far as the form of different *śabda*s is concerned, there are two sides[4] — *vyutpatti-pakṣa* and *avyutpatti-pakṣa*. The former, which is supported by Nairuktas and Śākaṭāyana, holds that all the nouns are formed by adding some *pratyaya* (suffix) or the other to a root of a verb whereas the latter

---

3. *siddhe śabdārthasambandhe lokoto 'rthaprayukte* ।
śabdaprayoge śāstreṇa dharmaniyamo yathā laukikavaidikeṣu ॥
— *Kātyāyanaḥ, Paspaśā, Mahābhāṣyam*

4. *nāma ca dhātujamāha nirukte, vyākaraṇe śakaṭasya ca tokam* ।
— *Vārtikam, uṇādayo bahulam, Pā.* 3-3-1

uṇādīnām pratiṣedho vaktavyaḥ, prātipadikavijñānācca bhagavataḥ pāṇineḥ siddham । — *Mahābhāṣyam, āyaneyī, Pā.* 7-1-2

ayāmantetisūtram pāṇinervyutpattipakṣasyāpisvīkāra ityasyāpi gamakam vyākaraṇāntararītyaiva . . . .
— *Laghuśabdenduśekharaḥ, Visargasandhiprakaraṇam*

holds that readymade *śabda*s are used. Bhartṛhari in Brahmakāṇḍa of *Vākyapadīyam*[5] explains that the things offered in Vyākaraṇa (derivations, etc.) are simply devices, which are designed to deceive the learner; rather they are wrong routes which ultimately lead to the right destination (a child is frightened/attracted through falsehoods in order to make it eat the food). The import is that the form of a *śabda* stands firm, in spite of the fact that the exploded view or *prakṛtipratyayavibhāga* offered may differ from Vyākaraṇa to Vyākaraṇa. Some Vaiyākaraṇas said that *pacati* is a conglomeration of *pac+a+ti*, whereas others offered *pac+ati*, as the derivation.

In spite of the fact that Pāṇini tried his best to exhibit the derivation of many words and even accepted *uṇādi*s as a supplement, Nāgeśabhaṭṭa, considered to be the best authority on *Pāṇinīya*, established, quoting Patañjali, that Pāṇini favours *avyutpatti-pakṣa* (Udyota 7-1-2 & *Śabdenduśekhara*).

The term *śabda* has got many meanings, viz. *mahāvākyam, avāntaravākyam, vākyam, padam, prakṛtiḥ, pratyayaḥ, varṇaḥ, parā, paśyantī, madhyamā, vaikharī, dhvaniḥ* and *śabdapramāṇam*. Therefore it is untranslatable. Before going to discuss each of the above items in detail let us have a glance at the hierarchy of the same.

Mahāvākyam or Discourse, is a group of ***avāntara-vākyas*** (sub-sentences) intended to transform a longer meaning. In other words, it corresponds to a sentence (*vākyam*) which is used to transform a meaning that is shorter.

Vākyam is a group of words (*padam*) which can render a unitary meaning. *Ākāṅkṣā* (mutual expectancy), *yogyatā*

---

5. *upāyāḥ śikṣamāṇānām bālānāmapalālanāḥ* ।
asatye vartmani sthitvā tatassatyaṁ samīhate ॥
— *Vākyapadīyam*, 2-238

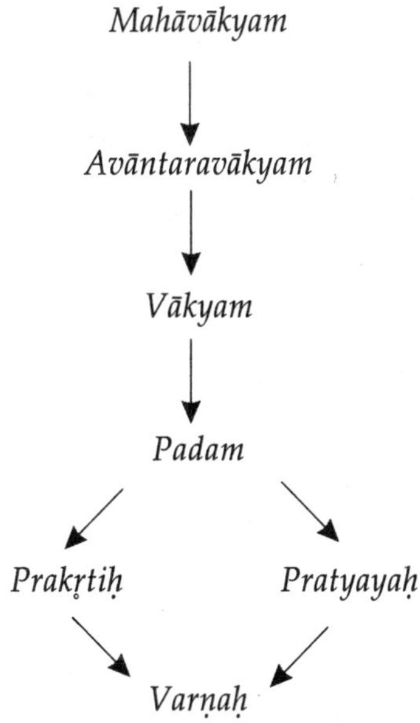

(compatibility) and *āsatti* (proximity) are the prerequisites for both a *mahāvākya* and a *vākya*.

Padam, is a conglomeration of *prakṛti* and *pratyaya* (root and suffix), which can be used independently. ***Prakṛti*** is the root both verbal and nominal. ***Pratyaya*** is the one that is added to a *prakṛti*. Neither *prakṛti* nor *pratyaya* can be employed independently.[6] ***Varṇa*** is the minimum unit that cannot be used independently.

It may be noted that the first two (*vākyam* and *padam*) are used/known to common people whereas *varṇa* is learnt in the alphabet. *Prakṛti* and *pratyaya* are exclusively useful for grammatical analysis (and they are in fact, artificial).

6. *na kevalā prakṛtiḥ prayoktavyā nāpi pratyayaḥ* ।
— *Vā/Bhā, arthavat Pā.* 1-2-45, *sarūpāṇāṁ Pā.* 1-2-64, *anabhihite Pā.* 2-3-1

It is a matter of concern that the linguists from the West have not adequately endeavoured to know as to whether there was any work done in the Eastern hemisphere, precisely the Indian subcontinent, before they started to write down the theories of language which were to be revised time and again. This point would be discussed in detail in the later part of this book.

The term "Oriental Theories" in this work refers to the ones propounded and expounded by Indian intelligentsia, rather the sages of Indian soil (Jaimini, Pāṇini, etc.) since time immemorial.

It was several thousands of years ago that the founders and propagators of different schools of Indian philosophy (including Vyākaraṇa and Alaṁkāra) had tried their best to compose large treatises, that contained theories, analyses, etc. in regard to language in general and Sanskrit in particular.

The concepts originated on Indian soil chiefly differ with the ones that are from Western hemisphere in one aspect — the former discuss language in both spiritualistic and materialistic terms whereas the latter are concerned only about their materialistic value. The Indian sages believed that the use of (perfect) *śabdas*, i.e. acceptable to Vyākaraṇam, fetches *dharma* and the abuse of language (or use of imperfect *śabdas*) would attract *adharma*. So much so that the user of the language (Sanskrit) should see to it that not only he transforms the intended meaning to the listener but also attains *dharma* (at the same time) which would ultimately help in achieving *mokṣa*.[7]

7. *siddhe śabdārthasambandhe lokoto 'rthaprayukte śabdaprayoge śāstreṇa dharmaniyamo yathā laukikavaidikeṣu* ।

— *Kātyāyanaḥ, Paspaśā, Mahābhāṣyam*

śabdabrahmaṇi niṣṇātaḥ param brahmādhigacchati ।

— *Bhāratam, Śāntiparvaḥ*, 232-30

→

Mahāvākya[8] or discourse is the largest unit of a linguistic composition. It contains more than one sentence and each sentence can render an incomplete meaning. Therefore, it can be said that each and every sentence in a discourse possesses the phenomenon of mutual expectancy. Such sentences are called *avāntaravākya*s or sub-sentences. The sub-sentence in a discourse corresponds to a word in a sentence. All the three prerequisites of a sentence, viz. *ākāṅkṣā* (mutual expectancy), *yogyatā* (compatibility) and *āsatti* (proximity) — are invariably required in a *mahāvākya* also. In a sentence like *caitraḥ gacchati* (Caitra is going), the word *caitraḥ* expects the other word *gacchati* to satisfy the *ākāṅkṣā* — what is he doing? Similarly, the word *gacchati* expects the other word *caitraḥ* to put to rest the *ākāṅkṣā* — who is going? This is called mutual expectancy. On the other hand, a group of words like *gauḥ, brāhmaṇaḥ hastī* cannot be called a sentence as none of the words has got the above-said phenomenon.

Agninā siñcati (watering with fire) is an example wherein one finds the absence of the phenomenon *yogyatā*. *Agni* does not possess the property that is useful for quenching, so much so that although the above sentence is syntactically right, it fails on semantic front and hence it cannot be employed.

→ *iyaṁ sā mokṣamāṇānāmajihmā rājapaddhatiḥ* ।
— *Vākyapadīyam*, 1-16

ūrdhvabāhurviraumyeṣa na hi kaścicchr̥ṇoti mām । *dharmādarthaśca kāmaśca sa dharmaḥ kiṁ na sevyate* ।*vāsaḥ vācā dharmamavāpnuhi* ।
— *Rāmāyaṇam*, 5-39-10

8. *vākyoccayo mahāvākyam, yogyatākāṅkṣāsattiyukta eva, yathā rāmāyaṇabhārataraghuvaṁśādi.* — *Sāhityadarpaṇam*, 2-1

sāpekṣā ye tu vākyārthāḥ padārthaireva te samāḥ ।
— *Vākyapadīyam*, 2-325

arthaikatvādekam vākyam sākāṅkṣam cedvibhāge syāt ।
— *Mīmāṁsādarśanam*, 2-1-14-46

Āsatti (proximity) is the use of words in a sentence in quick succession. If the speaker says *caitraḥ* now and *gacchati* after an hour or so, the listener would not be in a position to understand the full meaning. Therefore, there should not be too much gap in between while uttering the words of a sentence.

Similarly, a sub-sentence like "long long ago there was a king called Daśaratha" expects another sub-sentence, and the latter expects still another. Thus, the expectancy goes on till the end of the discourse — it can be a story, a description, a conversation — any stretch of language beyond a sentence. *Yogyatā* and *āsatti* also apply automatically.

The term *mahāvākya* conforms to meaning — a great sentence. The greatness, rather vastness is generally depending on *śabda*.

But people, who are acquainted with Indian philosophy, especially Vedānta school, are reminded of the (twelve) *mahāvākyas*, viz. *tat-tvam-asi*, etc. as soon as one utters the term *mahāvākya*. But most of them do not know that it is a *saṁjñā* (name) of secondary importance given depending on the load of the meaning such a sentence bears. Since the Upaniṣadic sentence is pregnant with the meaning of the entire Upaniṣad (i.e. the general meaning derived out of such a sentence is not the absolute meaning of the same, there is much more) and therefore it is the *artha-gaurava* (vastness of meaning) rather than *śabda-gaurava* (vastness of *śabda*) that prompted the sages to style such sub-sentences as *mahāvākyas*. I would touch this point again.

The concept is widely discussed in my first work, viz. *Mahāvākyavicāraḥ* (1986). A brief account is being provided here.

As has already been mentioned, Sanskrit language can be divided into two depending on the form (and accent but not meaning)[9] of the *śabdas*. It is Pūrva-Mīmāṁsā (also called Mīmāṁsā/Pūrvatantra/Vākyaśāstra) which exclusively deals with the exegeses of the former part of Vedas, viz. Mantra and Brāhmaṇa. (Uttara-Mīmāṁsā or Vedānta analyses the latter part, viz. Upaniṣads, the names conform to meaning.)

The founder of the available Mīmāṁsā is Jaimini (Patañjali records there was a Mīmāṁsa compiled by Kāśakṛtsnī — *kāśakṛtsninā proktā mīmāṁsā kāśakṛtsnī* — *Mahābhāṣya*, 4/1/14). He defined a *vākya*[10] thus — it is a *vākya* if there is unity of meaning (among the parts) and/or if a single thing is being proposed and if there is mutual expectancy when separated (*artha* in the *sūtra* means "meaning" and "purpose"). This definition invariably applies to both a *vākya* and *mahāvākya* (that's why Jaimini did not incorporate the word *padam* in the *sūtra*). Except in a few instances, the term *vākya* is used even for *mahāvākya* as the latter is popular in Upaniṣadic *mahāvākyas*.[11] The above definition, wherein the other prerequisites, viz. *yogyatā* and *āsatti* are implied, is applicable to both Vedic and secular discourses.

Types of Discourse

There are three types of Discourses in Sanskrit literature, viz. Vedic, Metalinguistic and Classical.

---

9. *yeṣu yeṣu artheṣu loke śabdāḥ prayujyante teṣvevārtheṣu vede 'pi śabdāḥ prayujyante* — *Śābarabhāṣyam*, 1-1-1-1
indraśatrurityādau veda eva na kāvye svaro viśeṣapratītikṛt — *Kāvyaprakāśaḥ*, 2-19

10. *arthaikatvādekam vākyam sākāṅkṣam cedvibhāge syāt* — *Mīmāṁsādarśanam*, 2-1-14-46
vākyam dvividham, mahāvākyam cāvāntaravākyam ceti — *Bālamīmāṁsāprakāśaḥ*

11. *pratyagātmani ativyāptivāraṇāya mahāvākyārthe vākyaśabdaḥ prayujyate* — *Nyāyavārtikatātparyapariśuddhiḥ*

DISCOURSE IN VEDIC LITERATURE

The Vedic literature can chiefly be divided into two parts — the *mantra — brāhmaṇa-bhāga* and *upaniṣad-bhāga*. In the former one we find two types of Discourses — the first one formed by the conglomeration of Injunctive sentences and commending or condemning sentences (commonly called *arthavāda*s). Jaimini's maxim clarifies that the *arthavāda* sentences would not go in vain. They are to be construed along with the Injunctive sentence.

The second type is formed by the federation of the principal sentence, which tells about the result of the ritual and the subordinate sentences, which explain as to how to perform the ritual. Jaimini, Śabara, Kumārila, Prabhākara, etc. the founders and propagators of Pūrva-Mīmāṁsā or Vākyaśāstra (the science of sentence) as it is widely known, had explained in detail the Theories of Discourse in their works. Pūrva-Mīmāṁsā was the pioneer in this regard.

In Upaniṣadic literature, the sentences which render the gist of a particular Upaniṣad such as *tat-tvam-asi* are called *mahāvākya*s. In fact, the entire Upaniṣad itself is a Discourse, since we find syntactical and logical connection among the minor sentences of an Upaniṣad. So that each Upaniṣad, which is similar to a story, can be taken as a Discourse. It may be noted that the general definition of a Discourse does not apply in respect of the famous *mahāvākya*s.

METALINGUISTIC DISCOURSE (DISCOURSE IN TECHNICAL JARGON)

This can be found in Śāstric and Dārśanic treatises like *Aṣṭādhyāyī* of Pāṇini, *Mīmāṁsādarśanam* of Jaimini, etc. Every maxim (or *sūtra*) in these treatises is a sub-sentence. While pronouncing the maxims, brevity is considered to be the most important factor. Therefore, one has to supplement the *sūtra* with some words to make it render a finite sense and thus the sub-sentence is formed. A sub-sentence is one which renders a complete meaning, by itself, but is a part of a Discourse (a group of maxims). And, hence, it can be stated that the Śāstric and Dārśanic treatises are constructed depending upon the Theory of Discourse. As the words like *guṇa, vṛddhi*, etc. give a meaning other than they do in common parlance this Discourse is different from the classical or spoken one.

DISCOURSE IN CLASSICAL SANSKRIT

It is clearly defined and illustrated by Viśvanātha, and all the epics and *kāvya*s fall under this category. Some Rhetoricians had used the words *vākyam* and *śabda* to denote a Discourse. It may be noted that there are similarities between the Vedic Discourse (type I) and the present one. A good chunk of material in the epics and *kāvya*s is devoted to commending the hero and his deeds, and condemning the villain. And there are also the important 18 descriptions of various things. All the sub-sentences which result either in commendation or condemnation are akin to *arthavāda*s in Vedic Discourse. Moreover, according to the desire of the speaker even a paragraph or a description or any portion of a larger treatise can be taken as a Discourse.

Let us see as to how various systems/schools of Indian philosophy have taken up the concept and elaborated.

Pūrva-Mīmāṁsā

In fact, the above-quoted definition of Maharṣi Jaimini was said/is useful to measure the length of a *Yajus* (*yajuḥparimāṇa*). Nevertheless, the maxim is composed in such a way that it is capable to define/analyse a sentence and a Discourse. This is clearly stated by Kumārila,[12] in *Tantravārtika* under the same *sūtra*. The term *sūtra* literally means string/thread. It conforms to meaning — the *sūtra*s are to be strung together whereby a Discourse is formed — and the same in turn is useful to analyse a Discourse. The former would be metalinguistic in nature. Śaṅkarācārya[13] clearly says that the task of *Vedāntasūtra*s is to string together the flowers called *Vedāntavākya*s. This is true in case of *sūtra*s in other Śāstras as well. A *sūtra* is an elliptical (sub) sentence (*vākyaikadeśa* or *avāntaravākya*). On the other hand, Kumārilabhaṭṭa[14] taking the cue from Pāṇini's *Aṣṭādhyāyī* explains as to how the *sūtra*s are put to use — "each and every *sūtra* gets united (*ekavākyatā*/one sentenceness) with other *sūtra*s, which are at other places and render the *upadeśa* (the unitary meaning) especially in Vyākaraṇa. . . ."

Arthaikatva or *ekavākyatā* (unity of sense or purpose/one-sentenceness/cohesion/coherence) is the criterion of both a *vākya* as well as a *mahāvākya* — the difference is that there will

---

12. *yajurbhedam ca muktvaitadvākyaikatvasya lakṣaṇam* ।
mantrabrāhmaṇalokeṣu vaktavyam kvopayujyate ॥
— *Tantravārtikam*, 2-1-14-46

13. *vedāntavākyakusumagrathanārthatvādvedāntasūtrāṇām* ।
— *Śāṅkarabhāṣyam*, 1-1-4

14. *sarvāṇyeva hi śāstrāṇi svapradeśāntaraissaha* ।
ekavākyatayā yuktamupadeśam pratanvate ॥

viśeṣeṇa tu vyākaraṇe । *tatra hyekaikasmin prāyeṇāṣṭādhyāyī vyāpriyate* । *iha caitāvatā pratyayavidhiḥ paripūryate* । *pratyayaḥ, paraśca, ādyudāttaśca, anudāttau suppitau, dhātoḥ, tatropapadam saptamīstham, kṛdatiṅ, vāsarūpo 'striyām, vartamāne laṭ, kartari kṛt, laḥ karmaṇi ca bhāve cākarmakebhyaḥ, lasya tibādayaḥ, anudātta ṅita ātmanepadam, śeṣātkartari parasmaipadam, yuṣmadasmadupapadādiṣu, madhyamādayaḥ, tiṅasstrīṇi trīṇi prathamamadhyamottamāḥ, tānyekavacanadvivacanabahuvacanānyekaśaḥ, bahuṣu bahuvacanam, dvyekayordvivacanaikavacane iti parāṇi ca saṁjñāparibhāṣādiśāstrāṇi sarvāṇyekam vākyam* । — *Tantravārtikam*, 3-4-4-13

be *padaikavākyatā* (one-sentenceness among words) in a *vākya* and *vākyaikavākyatā* (one-sentenceness among sub-sentences) in a *mahāvākya*.

There is not any limit so far as the length of a *mahāvākya*[15] is concerned. As long as the *vākyaikavākyatā* continues to penetrate the entire stretch it is considered to be a *mahāvākya*. This is clearly stated by both Kumārilabhaṭṭa, the founder of Bhāṭṭa school and Prabhākara Guru, the founder of Prābhākara school in *Tantravārtika* and *Bṛhatī* respectively.

On the other hand, Mīmāṁsakas declared that it is a defect called *vākyabheda*[16] to treat a *vākya/mahāvākya* into two, when there is *arthaikatva*. When there are two things to be proposed or two unrelated *vidhi*s (Injunctions) then there can be two *vākyas/mahāvākyas* — says Śabarasvāmī. It may be noted that Vaiyākaraṇas take this as a guideline in splitting the *sūtra*s of Pāṇini, called *yogavibhāga*. Pāṇini incorporated the term *tamaḥ* in *sthāne 'ntaratamaḥ* (1-1-50) to suggest *vākyabheda*. More on this aspect can be had from *Nyāsa, Pradīpa, Śabdakaustubha, Udyota*, etc.

---

15. *tasmātpadeṣu yāvatsu śrūyamāṇeṣu dṛśyate* ।
vispaṣṭamaikyamarthasya tāvatāmekavākyatā ॥
— *Tantravārtikam*, 2-1-14-46

ekatve hi na vākyaikatva evāvasthitiḥ, kintu sarvavākyānāmekavākyatā prāpnoti varṇānāmiva pade padānāmiva vākye. kasmāt? ekatvāvagamādeva । *bhavati hi sarvavākyeṣu śabdaḥ śabda ityeṣā buddhiḥ, sarvavākyārtheṣu ca śabdārthaḥ śabdārtha iti ca* । *tadidamabhinnameva jyotiṣṭomādi karmajātam prāpnoti* । — *Bṛhatī*, 1-1-5-5

16. *sambhavatyekavākyatve vākyabhedastu neṣyate* ।
— *Ślokavārtikam, Pratyakṣasūtram*, ślo : 9

arthabhedādvākyabhedaḥ, dvayośca vidhīyamānayoḥ parasparenāsambaddhayoḥ vākyabhedaprasaṅgaḥ, anekavidhito hi vākyabhedа uktaḥ ॥ — *Śābarabhāṣyam*, 3-2-10-27, etc.

The *ekavākyatā* among *avāntaravākyas* can be achieved through certain devices (according to Mīmāṁsakas), viz. *aṅgāṅgi-bhāva* (the relation of constitute and constituent), *śeṣa-śeṣi-bhāva* (the relation of complete and complement), *guṇa-guṇi-bhāva* (the relation of principal and subordinate) and *upakāryopakāraka-bhāva* (the relation of helper and helped). All these relations are reflected at linguistic level as *viśeṣaṇa-viśeṣya-bhāva* (the relation of qualifier and qualified). The following background is a must before we start any discussion on *ekavākyatā* and its basis.

We come across five types of sentences in Vedic Literature[17] — *vidhi, mantra, niṣedha, arthavāda* and *nāmadheya*. *Arthavāda* and *nāmadheya vākyas* are not independently authoritative. They are construed along with *vidhi-vākyas*, which are independently authoritative. *Mantra-vākyas* are useful in rites/sacrifices and are invariably taken with the *vidhi*. *Niṣedha-vākyas*, like *vidhi-vākyas*, are authoritative on their own. The sentences related to *parakṛti* and *purākalpa* are considered to be *arthavādas*.[18] Jaimini wrote *sūtras* to this effect in the sixth *adhyāya*. Similarly, the *phalaśruti*, which is there in *dravya, saṁskāra* and *karma*, also

---

17. *vidhiḥ* — Injunctive sentence
mantraḥ — The sacred formulas
niṣedhaḥ — The censuring sentence
arthavādaḥ — Sentences of commendation and condemnation
nāmadheyaḥ — Designation

— *Vājapeyādhikaraṇam*

18. *parakṛtiḥ* — The incident/story which has got a single *kartā*
purākalpaḥ — The incident/story where there are more than one *kartā*
phalaśrutiḥ — The paragraphs, generally found towards the end, wherein the result/fruit/benefit of performing such a rite/sacrifice is described.

falls under the heading *arthavāda* as the same are not *vidhi*s in that they are not directly useful in attaining the *puruṣārtha*, but are useful in sacrifice.

Mīmāṁsakas had enumerated six factors[19] that are helpful in understanding the meaning of *vidhi* (*niṣedha* is also a kind of *vidhi*) — *śruti, liṅga, vākya, prakaraṇa, sthāna* and *samākhyā*. Each of them is stronger than the latter and weaker than the former.

Among the said means the *vākya* through *prakaraṇa* which is in the form of *ubhayākāṅkṣā* (mutual expectancy), renders a unitary meaning. It is of two types — *mahāvākya* and *avāntara-vākya*. *Samabhivyāhāro vākyam* (a compact expression is a sentence) — is the definition generally offered by later Mīmāṁsakas. The words in a sentence become a compact expression on account of their conveying a unitary meaning. Similarly, the sub-sentences or *avāntaravākya*s in a macro-sentence (discourse) or *mahāvākya* together become a compact expression on account of their communicating a unitary meaning. The sub-sentences in a *mahāvākya* are akin to words in a *vākya*.

According to Mīmāṁsakas, the *vākya* is of the nature of *bhāvanā*, an urge — which is mainly expressed by a verb (in injunctive mood). Hence, the *vidhi-vākya* becomes the principal sentence and all other related sentences become subordinate.

---

19. *śrutiḥ* — Express Vedic statement
liṅgaḥ — Indication
vākyam — Syntactically connected sentence
prakaraṇam — Mutual expectancy
sthānam — Position
samākhyā — Juxtaposition

Śrutiliṅgavākyaprakaraṇasthānasamākhyānāṁ samavāye pāradaurbalyamarthaviprakarṣāt
— *Jaiminisūtram* 3-3-7-14

Unity in a macro-sentence at the expression level is achieved in two ways. A word may unite with a sentence to form a macro-sentence, i.e. *padaikavākyatā* (which is generally seen in a sentence). A (sub) sentence may also unite with another (sub) sentence to form a unit. Then it is called *vākyaikavākyatā*.

According to Mīmāṁsā,[20] the words denote their respective meanings. Then the *padārtha*s (word-meanings) unite to render the *vākyārtha*. So, all the words in a given situation form into a unitary sentence in so far as they have the same purpose.[21] This is as much true in common parlance as it is in the case of determination of the size of *Yajus*.[22] It is rightly said that if the meaning is not complete or the desired purpose is not served, we should take into consideration even the passages in other *śākhā*s of the Veda to complete the *mahāvākya*. The capacity of Veda (*veda-śakti*) is such, asserts Kumārila,[23] that in case the relevant material is not found in proximity (i.e. *ākāṅkṣā* is not satisfied) then its tentacles would permeate into material that is at a far away place (*śākhā* or chapter) and the same is an authority in uniting the factors — helper and helped — to make a *mahāvākya*. In Vyākaraṇa also *sūtra*s in different *adhyāya*s get united.

---

20. *padebhyaḥ padārthāḥ jāyante, padārthebhyo vākyārthāvagamaḥ* ।
— *Śabarasvāmī*, 1-1-1-1

21. *arthaikatvādekaṁ vākyam sākāṅkṣam cedvibhāge syāt* ।
— *Mīmāṁsādarśanam*, 2-1-14-46

22. *yajurbhedaṁ ca muktvaitadvākyaikatvasya lakṣaṇam* ।
mantrabrāhmaṇalokeṣu vaktavyam kvopayujyate ॥
— *Tantravārtikam*, 2-1-14-46

23. *yathā yathā hi sannikṛṣṭam na labhyate tathā tathā viprakṛṣṭe vedaśaktiḥ saṁcarati tadihopakārakalpanāpramāṇam* । *tena śākhāntaroktānāmapyaṅgānām pradhānavākyena samabhivyāhāraḥ* ।
— *Tantravārtikam* 3-3-4-11

The *avāntaravākyas* which can render a unitary meaning by themselves get united (*vākyaikavākyatā*) on account of their relation of principal and subordinate — says Kumārila.[24] So the unity of a sentence extends to all words that are required to make a complete sense. This unity of *avāntara-vākyas* in a *mahāvākya* is just like that of letters in a word and words in a sentence.

The unity at the linguistic level may be reflecting in having the same *vibhaktis*[25] (concord/congruence) or by way of the relation of *kriyā* and *kāraka* (the verb and the case) or by way of the complete and the complement — *nekṣetodyantamādityam*[26] (*na — īkṣeta — udyantam — ādityam* — one should not stare at the rising sun) — is an example. The negative particle is required to complete the *mahāvākya*. If we take the rest of it only, it is not authentic. The negative particle is invariably required to complete the sense. Kumārila[27] illustrates this with the example of a smaller number in a larger number (7, 946, 358 is a *mahāsaṁkhyā*, 79/46/358, etc. are *avāntara-saṁkhyas* and the latter are not authentic). If the *avāntaravākya*, however, is a

---

24. *svārthabodhe samāptānāmaṅgāṅgitvavyapekṣayā* ।
vākyānāmekavākyatvam punassamhatya jāyate ॥
— *Tantravārtikam*, 1-3-13-24

25. *ekavākyatā ca sati viśeṣaṇaviśeṣyabhāve bhavati, nānyathā* । *so 'pi ca sāmānādhikaraṇyena bhavati samānavibhaktyantānām, vaiyadhikaraṇyena vā kriyākārakarūpaḥ śeṣaśeṣirūpaśca* ।
— *Tantravārtikam*, 3-4-4-13

26. *na ca mahāvākye sati avāntaravākyam pramāṇam bhavati, padāntarasya bādhanāt, yathā nodyantamādityamīkṣeta iti pratiṣedho gamyate mahāvākyāt, avāntaravākyādīkṣaṇa-vidhānam* ।
— *Śābarabhāṣyam*, 6-4-7-25

27. *sarvatrāvāntaravākyāni mahāvākyeṣvapramāṇam, mahāsamkhyāsvivāvāntarasaṁkhyā bhavati* ।
— *Tantravārtikam*, 1-2-1-7

vidhi-vākya, it is authentic in itself, it does not require the help of others — *raktaḥ paṭo bhavati* (there is a red cloth) — is an example offered by Śabarasvāmī.[28] When there is a sentence like *paṭo bhavati* both these words do not have any kind of expectancy of another word. But when another word like *rakta* is heard, then there will be *ākāṅkṣā* with the word (*paṭaḥ*). Likewise, where there are no any kind of *arthavāda*s there *codanā/pracodanā* (urge) would be created (in the reader's mind) by *vidhi-vākya* only. On the other hand, if it is followed by *arthavāda*, then the *vidhi-arthavāda* combine would effect the *codanā* (in this context the term *avāntaravākyam* is used in the sense of *vākyam* without any qualifiers).

The entire range of sentences can precisely be put under the two headings — *vidhi* and *niṣedha*. Rather, it won't be amiss to say that either directly or indirectly all the sentences/ discourses propose *vidhi*. It is so because *niṣedha* is also a kind of *vidhi*. Śabarasvāmī clearly says — a condemnation is not being used to condemn the thing/person in question (Rāvaṇa,

---

28. *yathā paṭo bhavatīti paṭa utpadyate ityarthaḥ* । *nirākāṅkṣam ca padadvayam* । *yadā ca tasminneva rakta ityaparam śrūyate tadā rāgasambandhī bhavatītyarthaḥ, bhavati ca raktam pratyākāṅkṣā* । *evam yadā na stutipadāni vidhiśabdenaiva tadā prarocanā, yadā stutivacanam tadā stavanena* । — *Śābarabhāṣyam*, 1-2-1-7
yogyapadāntarānuccāraṇena hi sarvavākyāni paryavasyanti । *tathā ca yatropalapsyante tatraikavākyatāṁ gamiṣyante* । *tadiha mahāvākyena vinā avāntaravākyasya prāmāṇyam tadabhāve tu netyetadāha — yadā na stutipadānīti* । *nanvevam satīti* । *yatra mahāvākyāvāntaravākyayoḥ phalam bhidyate yathā paṭabhavanarāgabhavane, tatraiva yuktamiha tvanatiriktārthasya sataḥ kimavāntaravākyanirākaraṇameva mahāvākyasya yuktam phalam? tadetadāha yasmin satyavidhāyakamavāntaravākyam bhavati mā bhūttanmahāvākyamiti* । *yo nāma vedasya kartā syāt sa evam paryanuyujyeta laghunopāyena siddhe kim mahāvākyamāśrayasīti* । *tadabhāvānna paryanuyogaḥ* ।
— *Tantravārtikam*, 1-2-1-7

Duryodhana, etc.) rather it is to (indirectly) praise the right thing/person. The suggestion is not the censure of the condemned but admiration of the other. This norm is called *nahinindānyāya*.[29]

Not a single Vedic word should go to waste as Veda itself ordains[30] — one should recite/study Veda. Therefore, in order to see that each and every sentence in Veda is meaningful/ useful either directly or indirectly, Mīmāṁsakas had devised several ways. *Upakramopasaṁhāra*[31] combine is also such a device — if the paragraph or group of *avāntara-vākyas* has got the same *upakrama* (introduction) and *upasaṁhāra* (conclusion), then that particular unit can be considered as a *mahāvākya*. The same ruling applies in secular things, i.e. books, theses, dissertations, reports, etc. as well. It has to be clarified in this context that there should be *upakrama* and *upasaṁhāra* which are similar and all the sub-sentences therein should have been aimed at producing the same, single result.

Since the analysis depending on the above-listed devices consumes many pages it is being illustrated briefly.

The following is a *vidhi-vākya* followed by an *arthavāda* of eulogistic nature in *Taittirīya Saṁhitā* (*Kṛṣṇa Yajurveda*)[32] — "one desirous of prosperity should sacrifice the animal *śveta*,

29. *na hi nindā nindyam ninditum prayujyate kim tarhi ninditāditarat praśaṁsitum* । *tatra na ninditasya pratiṣedho gamyate kintvitarasya vidhiḥ* ।
— *Śābarabhāṣyam*, 2-4-2-21

30. *svādhyāyo 'dhyetavyaḥ* । — *Taittirīyāraṇyakam*, 2-15

31. *vākyāni yāvadartham syuḥ guṇebhyaḥ phalakalpane* ।
ekopakramasaṁhārādekaṁ cedaṁ pratīyate ॥
— *Tantravārtikam*, 1-4-11-22

32. *vāyavyagguṁśvetamālabheta bhūtikāmaḥ, vāyurvai kṣepiṣṭhā devatā, vāyumeva svena bhāgadheyenopadhāvati sa evainam bhūtim gamayati* ।
— *Taittirīya Saṁhitā*, 2-1-1

dedicated to Vāyu, as Vāyu is the fastest deity, and has to go to Vāyu with his own fate for assistance, Vāyu only would lead him to prosperity." In this passage the first sub-sentence is a *vidhi-vākya* and the rest, as a whole, is an *arthavāda* intended to create an urge in the mind of the reader to perform the sacrifice dedicated to Vāyu.

Jaimini in his maxim says that since they are being construed along with the *vidhi-vākyas*, they (*arthavādas*) become a valid means of knowledge. Therefore, as they serve some purpose or the other (*stuti*/praise, etc.) they cannot be set aside as unmeaningful. It is depending on this maxim that the later commentators had considered *arthavādas* as *vidhiśeṣa*[33] (related to *vidhi*) and the relation between *vidhi* and *arthavāda* as *śeṣa-śeṣī-bhāva* (the relation between complete and complement). The relations are the criteria in federating the *avāntara-vākyas* and thus sustaining the *ekavākyatā* at intersentential level (*vākyaikavākyatā*).

In the present context, the entire *arthavāda* is replaced by the term *praśasta* (praiseworthy), and would be connected with the *vidhi-vākya*. Thus we get *praśastaḥ vāyavīyaḥ yāgaḥ kartavyaḥ* (the prosperous *vāyuyāga* is to be performed) — a *mahāvākya*. On the other hand, one can just modify the commending

33. *vidhinātvekavākyatvāt stutyarthena vidhīnām syuḥ* ।
— *Jaiminisūtram*, 1-2-1-7

yena vidhīyate tasya vākyaśeṣa arthavāda ityuktam ।
— *Śābarabhāṣyam*, 1-2-4-31

vākyaśeṣo hi sa (arthavādaḥ) bhavati vidhātavyasya ।
— *Śābarabhāṣyam*, 1-4-1-1

na tāvadarthavādatvaṁ vākyaśeṣatvābhāvāt ।
— *Tantravārtikam*, 1-4-1-1

vidhīyamānasya ca vākyaśeṣatvena stāvakaḥ arthavādo bhavati ।
— *Tupṭīkā*, 10-7-9-27

sentences (to satisfy the *kāraka* rules) and may constitute a *mahāvākyārtha* (without any loss of meaning). Thus — *yataḥ śīghrakārisvabhāvatayā śīghraphalapradaḥ vāyuḥ asya śvetapaśoḥ devatā tataḥ praśastamimam vāyudevatākam paśum aiśvaryakāmaḥ samspṛśet*.

The above shown path can be adapted in the analysis of larger discourses like *Mahābhārata*, *Rāmāyaṇa*[34] and other *mahāvākyas*, where one would find many *arthavādas*. In fact, Kumārila clearly says this in *Tantravārtikam* — thus discourses like *Mahābhārata* are to be analysed.

In the above example, the *vidhi-vākya* has got *ākāṅkṣā* — why should one sacrifice the *śveta* of which Vāyu is the deity? On the other side, the *arthavādas* have got the *ākāṅkṣā* — so what has to be done? Since there is *ākāṅkṣā* on both sides, and either can/would put to rest the *ākāṅkṣā* of the other, the combine of both the stretches can be/has to be taken as a *mahāvākya*. To put it in Mīmāṁsakas' words, the *vidhi-vākya* has got *itikartavyatākāṅkṣā* and one would get *prāśastyajñāna* from *arthavāda-vākyas*. That is how the *vākyaikavākyatā* becomes possible.

The *avāntara-vākya*, which denotes the *phala*/result is called *aṅgi-vākya* and naturally it would have an *ākāṅkṣā* called *kathambhāvākāṅkṣā* (how to attain this result?). On the other side, there will be some *avāntara-vākyas*, which would explain the way something has to be done, called *aṅga-vākyas* and naturally these would have the *phalākāṅkṣā* (what is the result of these rites?). Since there is *ākāṅkṣā* on both sides the passage falls under the *prakaraṇa*[35] and subsequently there will be

---

34. *evam bhāratādivākyāni vyākhyeyāni* ।
— *Tantravārtikam* 1-2-1-7

35. *ubhayākāṅkṣārūpam prakaraṇam* । — *Mīmāṁsānyāyaprakāśaḥ*

vākyaikavākyatā and thus a *mahāvākya* is formed. Such a *mahāvākya*, through the creation of *liṅga* and *śruti*,[36] generates *codanā* in the said sacrifice, in the mind of the reader — *darśapūrṇamāsābhyām svargakāmo yajeta*[37] (one desirous of heaven should sacrifice with *darśa* and *pūrṇamāsa* [new-moon-day and full-moon-day]) — this is an *aṅgi-vākya* and the same has got an *ākāṅkṣā*, i.e. how to perform the sacrifice? *Samidho yajati, tanūnapātam yajati*, etc. are *aṅga-vākya*s which have got the *phalākāṅkṣā*, i.e. what is the result of performing such rites? In such a situation, since there is *ākāṅkṣā* on both sides, i.e. *aṅga* and *aṅgi*, it has to be taken as a *prakaraṇa* and subsequently the *vākyaikavākyatā* is effected which would result in the formation of *mahāvākya* — *samidādyaṅgasahitābhyām darśapūrṇamāsābhyām svargakāmo yajeta* (one desirous of *svarga* should perform the *darśapūrṇamāsayāga* through *samit, tanūnapāt*, etc.).

It won't be amiss to take a *prakaraṇa* by putting together *aṅgi-vākya* and *aṅga-vākya* that are there at different places. This ruling more clearly applies in *Pāṇinīya*. Kumārilabhaṭṭa[38] offered a clarification in this regard — when one does not get the *aṅgi-vākya* and *aṅga-vākya* nearby each other then the *Veda-śakti* goes any far. This is how the helper and the helped (*upakārya* and *upakāraka*) are decided. Therefore, the *aṅgi-vākya* would get united with *aṅga-vākya*s of another *śākhā*. *Aṅgāṅgī-*

---

36. *ekavākyatayā yāvatsāmarthyamanumīyate* ।
sāmarthyena śrutistāvatkalpyate viniyojikā ॥
— *Tantravārtikam*, 3-3-7-14

37. *ya evam vidvān darśapūrṇamāsau yajate tābhyāmeva suvargam lokamanupaśyati* । — *Taittirīya-Saṁhitā*, 2-5-6

38. *yathā yathā hi sannikṛṣṭaṁ na labhyate tathā tathā viprakṛṣṭe vedaśaktiḥ saṁcarati tadihopakārakalpanāpramāṇam* । *tena śākhāntaroktānāmapyaṅgānām pradhānavākyena samabhivyāhāraḥ* ।
— *Tantravārtikam*, 3-3-4-11

bhāva can be effected in places when there is *upakāryopakāraka-bhāva*[39] or *śeṣa-śeṣī-bhāva.*[40]

Two famous commentators, viz. Bhaṭṭakumārila and Prabhākara, had taken different ways regarding the conception of the meaning of a *vākya/mahāvākya.*

Abhihitānvayavāda

Kumārila opines that initially words denote their meaning and then the meanings would get united and thus the *vākyārtha* is achieved (in case of *mahāvākya,* the *avāntara-vākyas* denote their meaning and then the meanings get united to achieve *mahāvākyārtha*). *Bhāvanā* or the meaning of the verb, supported by the *kārakas* and qualifiers is the *vākyārtha,* according to Mīmāṁsakas. Vaiyākaraṇas follow the same path. *Bhāvanāmukhyaviśeṣyakaśābdabodha* of the former is akin to *dhātvārthamukhyaviśeṣyakaśābdabodha* of the latter. While following the above path, at times, the Naiyāyikas advocate *prathamāntārthamukhyaviśeṣyakaśābdabodha* (the meaning of the

---

39. *upakārāpekṣāyām hi aṅgāni śrūyante* ।
— *Śābarabhāṣyam,* 11-1-1-6

40. *śeṣam tasyaiva taṁ vidyādupakāreṇa lakṣitam* ।
bhavatyevam ca homāderbhinnādi pratyaśeṣatā ॥

na hi bhinnopakārārthaḥ sa taddhyevopakārakam ।
vede ca nānyadaṅgatvakāraṇam dṛśyate kvacit ॥

evam sati pradhānānāmaṅgānām ca parasparam ।
aṅgāṅgānām ca sarveṣām saṁkīryetaiva śeṣatā ॥

pradhānānyapyato 'ṅgānāmaṅgāni syuranugrahāt ।
syādanyonyopakārācca teṣāmanyonyaśeṣatā ॥

naikenā 'pi pradhānena vinā 'nye sādhyate phalam ।
tenaitānyupakurvanti phalasiddhau parasparam ॥

upakāreṇa śeṣatvam, śeṣatvāccopakāritā ।
svātaṁtryeṇa prasiddham hi na hyanyataradetayoḥ ॥
— *Tantravārtikam,* 3-1-2-2

word in nominative case is qualified in the sentence meaning). The first two processes had their origin in Yāska's *Niruktam* — *bhāvapradhānamākhyātam, sattvapradhānāni nāmāni*. The above popular concepts were first mentioned by Gaṅgeśopādhyāya of eleventh century.

Anvitābhidhānavāda

Prabhākara holds that the words in a sentence would get united as per the *ākāṅkṣā* and *yogyatā* and render the meaning so that the *vākyārtha* is achieved.

Prabhākara[41] refutes the contention of Śabarasvāmī, that the last *varṇa*, supported by the *saṁskāra* of earlier *varṇa*s, is the candidate, which renders the *vākyārtha*, saying that it is not possible in the case of a *mahāvākya* and hence one has to resort to words.

The origin of both the above *vāda*s is the statement of Śabarasvāmī — *padebhyaḥ padārthāḥ jāyante, padārthebhyaḥ vākyārthāvagamaḥ* (word-meanings are produced from words, through them sentence-meaning is understood).

Uttara-Mīmāṁsā (Vedānta)

As has been stated earlier, it was the famous twelve or so Upaniṣadic *mahāvākyas*[42] one would understand as soon as the term *mahāvākya* is uttered. Vedāntins follow in the footsteps of Mīmāṁsakas, so far as the *vākya* and *vākyārtha* are concerned.

---

41. *bhāṣyakāravacanam ca pūrvapūrva-varṇānujanitasaṁskāra-sahito 'ntyaḥ varṇaḥ pratyāyakaḥ iti nirviṣayam, aśakyam ca mahāvākyasya sakṛtsmaraṇam, tasmāt padānāmeva vācakaśakti-rāśrayaṇīyā* । — *Prakaraṇapañcikā*, 1-1-5

42. *tattvamasi* । — *Chāndogyopaniṣat*, 6-8-7
ayamātmā brahma । — *Bṛhadāraṇyakopaniṣat*, 11-5-19
aham brahmāsmi । — *Bṛhadāraṇyakopaniṣat*, 1-4-10

Different *ācāryas*, viz. Śaṅkara, Rāmānuja, Madhva, Vallabha, etc. had commented on *Brahmasūtras* of Veda-Vyāsa in accordance with their theme, i.e. Advaita, Viśiṣṭādvaita, Dvaita, etc. But all of them should/do accept that the gamut of Upaniṣads has its purport in only one thing, viz. *Brahman*. Śaṅkarācārya under *Janmādisūtra* says that the very purpose of *Vedāntasūtras* (*sūtra* means a string/thread) is federating/ stringing together the flowers of Vedānta-*vākyas* and the Vedānta-*vākyas* are being discussed by *sūtras* with examples.

The Vedānta-*vākyas* are construed with each other in order to establish *Brahman*. *Tattu samanvayāt* (1-1-4) says Veda-Vyāsa in *Brahmasūtras*. The term *tat* anywhere in Vedānta means *Brahman*. *Samanvaya* derivatively means well knitting. So much so that the *Brahman* can be established through well knitting of Vedānta-*vākyas* — turns out to be the meaning of the *sūtra*.[43] The Vedānta *vākyas* have to be connected in such a way so that the purport would be *Brahman*. Originally, it was in *Bṛhat Saṁhitā*[44] (not available?) that the six deciding factors of *tātparya*/purport were enumerated and all the commentators had followed suit — *upakrama* and *upasaṁhāra* (the beginning and the end or introduction and conclusion), *abhyāsa* (repetition), *apūrvatā* (novelty), *phala* (purpose), *arthavāda* (praise) and *upapatti* (argument). Among the said six factors, *phalam*, *apūrvatā* and *upapatti* are related to *artha* (meaning) and the rest to *śabda*.

Śaṅkara[45] says that mainly *upakrama* and *upasaṁhāra* are

---

43. *vedāntavākyakusumagrathanārthatvāt vedāntasūtrāṇām, vedānta-vākyāni sūtrairudāhṛtya vicāryante* I — *Śāṅkarabhāṣyam*, 1-1-4

44. *upakramopasaṁhārāvabhyāso 'pūrvatā phalam* I
arthavādopapattī ca liṅgam tātparyanirṇaye II
— *Bṛhat Saṁhitā* (*Sarvadarśanasaṁgrahaḥ*)

45. *upakramopasaṁhārābhyām hi vākyaikatvamavagamyate* I
— *Śāṅkarabhāṣyam*, 1-1-31

the factors which would decide the *vākyaikavākyatā* in an Upaniṣad, viz. *Chāndogya, Bṛhadāraṇyaka,* etc. Rāmānuja[46] also emphasizes in *Śrībhāṣya* that the Upaniṣadic sentences which have undergone the condition of *ekavākyatā* only are authentic. In Viyadadhikaraṇa of *Brahmasūtrabhāṣya,* Śaṅkara[47] goes one step ahead and clearly says that there is *ekavākyatā* among all the Śrutis (Vedas).

The sentences like *tat-tvam-asi* are loaded with cryptic meaning which is actually the gist of the entire Upaniṣad of which it is an integral part. Hence such sentences are styled *mahāvākyas,* i.e. the greatness/vastness is that of *artha* rather than *śabda* (a detailed account is available in my first book, *Mahāvākyavicāraḥ* 1986). It may not be amiss to generate *mahāvākya*s for *kāvya*s like *Rāmāyaṇa* and *Mahābhārata* — *rāmavadvartitavyam, na tu rāvaṇādivat* (one should emulate Rāma and not Rāvaṇa, etc.) can be a *mahāvākya,* which is the gist of *Rāmāyaṇa. Dharmarājādivadvartitavyam na tu duryodhanādivat* (one should emulate Dharmarāja, etc. and not Duryodhana, etc.) can be a *mahāvākya,* which is the gist of *Mahābhārata.*

In conclusion, as it is in the case of other Śāstras, in Vedānta also *sūtra*s would get united through *ekavākyatā.*

Vyākaraṇam I

The earlier discussion was almost entirely related to Vedic language. The theory of *mahāvākya* in *laukika bhāṣā* (secular language) is not adequately discussed in either Mīmāṁsā or Vedānta.

---

46. *tenaikavākyatāmāpannānyarthasadbhāve pramāṇam* I
— *Śrībhāṣyam,* 1-1-4

47. *ekavākyatvātsarvaśrutīnām* I
— *Śāṅkarabhāṣyam, Viyadadhikaraṇam*

Vyākaraṇa, Nyāya, Vaiśeṣika and Alaṁkāra are the systems wherein we come across a great deal of material related to the concept of *mahāvākya* in secular language. More or less all the above systems follow the Mīmāṁsā.

More conspicuous is the *ekavākyatā* in the *pāribhāṣika-bhāṣā* (technical/terminological language), i.e. the one among the *sūtra*s of Pāṇini. There are six types of *sūtra*s in *Aṣṭādhyāyī*[48] — *saṁjñā, paribhāṣā, vidhi, niyama, atideśa* and *adhikāra*. Since it is used directly in effecting the grammatical application, the *vidhisūtra* is considered to be the principal and the rest are subordinate as they play a secondary role in the application. Economy in the number of *sūtra*s is the reason behind such a system. As has already been mentioned, *sūtra* means an elliptical/incomplete sentence. The definition of a *sūtra* in *Parāśaropapurāṇa*[49] is as follows — the one (a sentence), brief with the least number of letters, unambiguous, strong enough, loaded with meaning, useful in innumerable cases, not so vast/lengthy and impeccable is a *sūtra* (in the verse *'vākyam'* is to be supplemented, otherwise it remains without a qualified). The *sūtra*s of Pāṇini are the best suited examples of the above definition.

As there is *aṅgāṅgi-bhāva* between the *aṅga*s and *aṅgi*, which are scattered across different *śākhā*s in Veda, in Vyākaraṇa too there will be *aṅgāṅgi-bhāva* among *sūtra*s strewn across *Aṣṭādhyāyī*. Bhartṛhari,[50] following Patañjali on *kartari kṛt* (3-4-

---

48. *saṁjñā ca paribhāṣā ca vidhirniyama eva ca* I
atideśo 'dhikāraśca sūtram ṣaḍvidham smṛtam II

49. *alpākṣaramasandigdham sāravadviśvatomukham* I
astobhamanavadyam ca sūtram sūtravido viduḥ II
— *Parāśaropapurāṇam & Viṣṇudharmottarapurāṇam*

50. *niyamaḥ pratiṣedhaśca vidhiśeṣasthatā sati* I
dvitīye yo lugākhyātastaccheṣamalukam viduḥ II
— *Vākyapadīyam*, 2-349

→

67), illustrates this aspect in *Vākyapadīyam* — the *niyama* and *pratiṣedha* are considered to be the complements of *vidhi* and therefore Vaiyākaraṇas say that the *aluk* in sixth *adhyāya* (*aluguttarapade* 6-3-1) is the complement of the *luk* in second *adhyāya* (*supo dhātuprātipadikayoḥ* 2-4-71)

Patañjali under *nājjhalan* explains[51] as to how a group of *sūtras* would serve the purpose — initially the alphabet (*aiuṇ, ṛḷk*, etc.) is learnt, then the *it saṁjñā* (through *upadeśe 'janunāsika it, halantyam*, etc.), then the *pratyāhāra* through *ādirantyena sahetā*, then the *savarṇa-saṁjñā* through *tulyāsyaprayatnam savarṇam*. By this united/unified sentence (*mahāvākya*) the *savarṇas* are taken elsewhere (not simply by the *sūtra-tulyāsyaprayatnam savarṇam*).

It was in order to exhibit the *ekavākyatā* between *vidhisūtra* on one side and other related *sūtras* on the other that Patañjali[52]

→ *videśasthamapi sadekam vākyam bhavati, tadyathā dvitīyādhyāye-lugucyate caturthaṣaṣṭhayoralugucyate 'pavādaḥ* ।
— *Mahābhāṣyam*, 3-4-67

51. *vākyāparisamāptervā punassiddhametat* । *kimidam vākyā-parisamāpteriti? varṇānāmupadeśastāvat upadeśottarakāletsaṁjñā itsaṁjñottarakāla ādirantyena sahetā iti pratyāhāraḥ pratyāhārottarakālā savarṇasaṁjñā savarṇasaṁjñottarakālam aṇuditsavarṇasya cāpratyaya iti savarṇagrahaṇam etena sarveṇa samuditena vākyenānyatra savarṇānām grahaṇam bhavati* । — *Mahābhāṣyam*, P 1-10

52. *uddeśam upadeśadeśam anatikramya yathoddeśam* ।
kāryeṇa vidhisūtreṇa kālyate ākṛṣyate iti kāryakālaḥ ॥
— *Mahābhāṣyam*, 1-1-11

(*yathoddeśapakṣe samjñāparibhāṣāsūtradeśe eva vidhiśāstrāṇām saṁjñāparibhāṣāśāstraiḥ ekavākyatā* । *kāryakāle ca vidhipradeśe eva saṁjñāparibhāṣāsūtrāṇām vidhisūtreṇa sahaikavākyatā iti viśeṣaḥ*) *ayaṁ pakṣo yathāśrutagrāhipratipatrapekṣaḥ mahāvākyārthaparyālocana-pravṛttapratipatrapekṣastu kāryakālapakṣaḥ* । — *Pradīpaḥ*, 1-1-11

adhikāro nāma triprakāraḥ । *kaścidekadeśasthaḥ sarvam śāstramabhijvalayati yathā pradīpaḥ suprajvalitaḥ sarvam veśmābhijvalayati* ।
— *Mahābhāṣyam*, 2-1-1

kaścit paribhāṣārūpaḥ । — *Pradīpaḥ* 2-1-1

invented two devices — *yathoddeśa* and *kāryakāla*. The *guṇasūtras* (*saṁjñā* and *paribhāṣā*) render their meaning in their respective places and the related *vidhisūtras* come to that point for *saṁskāra* — *vṛddhirādaic* (1-1-1) is a *saṁjñā-sūtra*. It renders the meaning — *ā, ai* and *au* are called *vṛddhi*, then and there as was pronounced by Pāṇini. *Vṛddhireci* (6-1-88) is a *vidhi-sūtra*. For understanding the term *vṛddhi* we have to bring the same to *vṛddhirādaic*. Both the *adhikāra-sūtras*, i.e. *saṁhitāyām* and *ekaḥ pūrvaparayoḥ*, follow the *vidhi-sūtra*. Thus, we get the following *mahāvākyārtha* — in Saṁhitā if *a* is followed by *ec* (*e o ai au*), one of the *vṛddhi-varṇas*, i.e. *ā, ai, au* replaces both the *pūrva* and *para* vowels (ex : *kṛṣṇa* + *ekatvam* = *kṛṣṇaikatvam*). This is *yathoddeśapakṣa*.

Kāryakāla means attracting *guṇa-sūtras* by *vidhi-sūtra*. As per the restriction *pūrvatrāsiddham* (8-2-1 which says that the later *sūtras*, i.e. that are there in *Tripadī*, would disappear while an application instituted by earlier *sūtras*, i.e. that are there in *Sapādasaptādhyāyī*, is taken up, even in *Tripadī* the former prevails upon the latter) the *vidhi-sūtras* of *Tripadī* cannot be brought to *Sapādasaptādhyāyī* and hence *yathoddeśa* does not work. In *kāryakāla* all the required *saṁjñās* and *paribhāṣās* are brought to the *vidhi-sūtra* and then there will be *vākyaikavākyatā* among them.

Brevity is the purpose of *adhikāra-sūtras*. A single *sūtra* (*vibhāṣa, aṅgasya, padaṣya*, etc.) runs into many *vidhi-sūtras* and then and there only (not at the place it is pronounced) the *adhikāra-sūtra*, along with the *vidhi-sūtra* renders the meaning. In fact, *adhikāra* is also a kind of *paribhāṣā*. The difference is that *adhikāra* runs into certain specified number of *sūtras*, whereas *paribhāṣā*, like a lamp in a house, illuminates the entire Śāstra.

So far as the *apavāda-śāstras* are concerned, Patañjali[53] clarifies that it is *apavāda-śāstra* first and *utsarga-śāstra* next and not vice versa (*utsarga* is general rule, and *niṣedha* or *apavāda* is the exceptional one. *Sūtra* and *śāstra* are used as synonyms also. *Śāstra* means school/system). He rather questions the propriety/usefulness of *niṣedha* (*apavāda*) in case the *utsarga* is once applied. (It is something like asking somebody, who has already taken food, not to take). Therefore, according to Pāṇini the *utsarga-śāstra* is applicable in examples which are not subject to *niṣedha-śāstra* and not the other way round. Moreover, as it is in the case in day-to-day life (*loka*) one should be particular about the time/order, i.e. serve curd to brāhmaṇas but buttermilk to Kauṇḍinya — is a usage which would explain the situation clearly. Both the sub-sentences in the above macro-sentence should be uttered without pause/interval. Then only the listener would serve curd to all the brāhmaṇas except Kauṇḍinya, who is also a brāhmaṇa. Let us consider that in case the first sentence is uttered in the morning and the other in the afternoon, it won't serve the purpose — the curd is not replaced by buttermilk (in case of Kauṇḍinya, who was suffering from cold) — although Pāṇini said the *utsarga*

---

53. *prakalpya cāpavādaviṣayam tata utsargaḥ pravartate. yo hi bhuktavantam prati brūyāt mā bhukthā iti kim tena kṛtam syāt* ।

— *Mahābhāṣyam*, 3-4-67

utsargavākye yattyaktamaśabdamiva śabdavat ।
tadbādhakeṣu vākyeṣu śrutamanyatra gamyate ॥

— *Vākyapadīyam* 2-346

brāhmaṇānām śrutirdadhni prakrāntā māṭharam vinā ।
māṭharastakrasambandhāt tatrācaṣṭe yathārthatām ॥

— *Vākyapadīyam* 2-347

anekākhyātayoge 'pi vākyam nyāyāpavādayoḥ ।
ekameveṣyate kaiścidbhinnarūpamiva sthitam ॥

— *Vākyapadīyam*, 2-348

and *niṣedha* in different places (different times) the student should leave the restricted places and then only apply the *utsarga*, i.e. there will be *ekavākyatā* between the two. *Karmaṇyaṇ* (3-2-1) is an *utsarga-sūtra* and *āto 'nupasarge kaḥ* (3-2-3) is an *apavāda-śāstra*. Therefore, the *dhātus*, except those ending in *ā* and without a prefix, with a *karmavācaka* as *upapada* would get *aṇ-pratyaya* (in the exceptional cases it would be *ka-pratyaya*) — is the *mahāvākya* that emerges after effecting the *ekavākyatā*.[54] (In fact, the students of Indian philosophy, especially that of Vyākaraṇa should be taught this linguistic phenomenon. Unfortunately neither the present traditional nor the modern system refers to such an essential component, without which even a single application cannot be effected.)

As a matter of fact, the *ekavākyatā* in Vyākaraṇa is an *upalakṣaṇa* (example/more to be included) to other Śāstras.

Vyākaraṇam II

The Vaiyākaraṇas from Pāṇini downwards had discussed the form of a *mahāvākya*. It is not the task of Vaiyākaraṇas to define a *vākya/mahāvākya*. They borrowed the definition (common to both) offered by Jaimini. In the beginning of Vākyakāṇḍa of *Vākyapadīya*, Bhartṛhari summarized the various definitions of *vākya* of other systemists. Consequently, he discusses the concept of *akhaṇḍa-vākya* and the case of *mahāvākya* also. Mīmāṁsakas hold that a group of words is a *vākya* and that of sub-sentences (*avāntara-vākya*s) is a *mahāvākya*, whereas Vaiyākaraṇas hold that it is an *akhaṇḍa-vākya* or *akhaṇḍa-mahāvākya* and the words and *avāntara-vākya*s are carved from these respectively, and therefore are artificial. This aspect would be discussed in detail at a later stage.

---

54. *sarvāṇyeva hi śāstrāṇi svapradeśāntaraissaha* ।
ekavākyatayā yuktamupadeśam pratanvate ॥
— *Tantravārtikam*, 3-4-4-13

Pāṇini in third *adhyāya* registered the usage of — *lṛṭ* or *laṅ* while recollecting an experience — *vibhāṣā sākāṅkṣe* (3-2-112) is the *sūtra* which says that *lṛṭ* (or *laṅ*) is used if the meaning of the verb has got expectancy. The example, i.e. *abhijānāsi devadatta yatkaśmīreṣu vatsyāmaḥ tatrādhyeṣyāmahe* (do you remember Devadatta, we used to live in Kaśmīra and study there) — apparently is not a sentence but a group of two sub-sentences, which are coherent. *Na yadi* (3-2-113) is another example.

Bhartṛhari, in *Vākyapadīya* (Vākyakāṇḍa) discusses the concept of *mahāvākya* and at the same time clarifies the doubts raised by Mīmāṁsakas. While proposing the *akhaṇḍa-vākya* (*akhaṇḍa-mahāvākya*) Hari[55] gives the definition (in fact, offered by Mīmāṁsakas) of a *mahāvākya* — a group of sentences meant to render a single meaning or propose a single thing, where the parts thereof have got expectancy. Elsewhere, in the same context Hari[56] says that the *avāntara-vākyārtha*s (in a *mahāvākyārtha*) are akin to *padārtha*s (in a *vākyārtha*).

Under the headings — *ākāṅkṣā* and *tātparya*, Nāgeśabhaṭṭa[57]

---

55. *vākyānām samudāyaśca ya ekārthaprasiddhaye, sākāṅkṣāvayavaḥ . . .*
— *Vākyapadīyam*, 2-76

56. *sāpekṣā ye tu vākyārthāḥ padārthaireva te samāḥ* ।
— *Vākyapadīyam*, 2-325

57. *anvayabodhaśca tadākāṅkṣitasakalakriyākārakādiviṣayo vivakṣitaḥ* । *etena tasya hetutve khaṇḍavākyārthabodhottaram mahāvākyārthabodho na syādityapāstam* । *khaṇḍabodhasya kriyātadviśeṣaṇakārakatadviśeṣaṇaitadanyataramātraviṣayatvāt* । — *Laghumañjūṣā, Ākāṅkṣānirūpaṇam*

atra śrautatāvatpadārthajñānānām ākāṅkṣādijñānānām ca naṣṭatve 'pi teṣām samūhālambanasmaraṇāt tatsaṁskārādvā 'nvayabodhaḥ । *ayameva khalekapotanyāyena bodhaḥ* । *yadā tu krameṇaiva udbodhasamavadhānāttattatkhaṇḍavākyārthabodhottaram pūrvasmaraṇāt tatsaṁskārādvā mahāvākyārthabodhastadā rājapurapra-veśanyāyena bodhaḥ* । — *Laghumañjūṣā, Tātparyanirūpaṇam*

in *Laghumañjūṣā* explains that after understanding the *khaṇḍa-vākyas* (*avāntara-vākyas*) one would certainly get the *mahā-vākyārtha-bodha*. In such an understanding there are two Nyāyas — Khalekapotanyāya and Rājapurapraveśanyāya — according to the former one, all the doves/pigeons, i.e. the old, young and younger ones, alight on the thrashing floor simultaneously and in a similar manner the *jñāna*s (cognitions) of all the *khaṇḍa-vākya*s culminate simultaneously and thus a *mahā-vākyārtha-jñāna* is obtained. On the other hand, according to the latter it is how the people, who have got some business in the king's palace, enter by forming a queue rather than in an unorganized manner, that the *khaṇḍa-vākyārtha*s are understood one after another and thus a *mahā-vākyārtha-jñāna* is achieved.

Hari[58] elaborates the two aspects of *vākyaparisamāpti* of *mahāvākya*s that are proposed in *Mahābhāṣya* — *samudāye parisamāptam* and *pratyekam parisamāptam*. *Mahāvākya* is called by another name *aṅgi-vākya*. The *avāntara-vākya*s would become *aṅga-vākyas*. The *aṅgi-vākya* itself indicates the meaning of *aṅga-vākya*s also. Since it is important, *aṅgi-vākya* is called *mahāvākya*. The *aṅgi-vākya* would get connected to *aṅga-vākya*s separately and this is called *pratyekaparisamāpti*. When a single *mahāvākya* is going to indicate the meaning of the entire group of *avāntara-vākya*s then it is called *samudāyaparisamāpti*.

Rāmavadvartitavyam na tu rāvaṇādivat (one should emulate Rāma and not Rāvaṇa, etc.) is called a *mahāvākya* following *pratyekaparisamāpti*. All the *avāntara-vākya*s in *Rāmāyaṇa* would have their purport in this *mahāvākya*. Similarly, *dharmarājādivadvartitavyam na tu duryodhanādivat* (follow Dharmarāja, etc. and not

58. *vākyāntarāṇām pratyekam samāptiḥ kaiścidiṣyate* ।
rūpāntareṇa yuktānām vākyānām tena saṁgrahaḥ ॥
— *Vākyapadīyam*, 2-389

Duryodhana, etc.) is a *mahāvākya* of *Mahābhārata*. Every *mahākāvya* would have a *mahāvākya* like this and it gives the essence/gist of that particular *kāvya*. Here also, as it was in the case of Vedāntamahāvākyas, the name is given depending on *artha-gaurava* rather than *śabda-gaurava*.

Nyāya and Vaiśeṣika

Anumāna (inference) occupies an important role among all the *pramāṇas* (means of knowledge), viz. *pratyakṣa, anumāna, śabda* and *upamāna*, that were proposed in Nyāya and Vaiśeṣika *darśanas*. (For a detailed account of the subject refer to my forthcoming book *Pramāṇas in Indian Philosophy*.)

Anumāna[59] is of two types — *svārthānumāna* and *parārthānumāna*. One's own knowledge through *anumāna-pramāṇa* is called *svārthānumāna*. When someone with *svārthānumāna* wants to produce the inferential knowledge in the mind of another man he employs five *avāntara-vākyas*. This is called *parārthānumāna* (derivatively an *anumāna* intended for others).

The knowledge related to a *parokṣa-vastu* (of a thing that cannot be perceived) that is produced through the five members/*avayavas* (of the syllogistic discourse) is generally called *anumāna*. There is smoke emanating from fire in a kitchen; no smoke is emanating from a hot iron ball; nor is there any smoke in a lake where there is no fire at all — one would have all these experiences and decides — wherever there is smoke there is fire; there is no smoke everywhere where there is fire; and there is no smoke anywhere where there is no fire at all. Such a person observes smoke emanating on a hill at a far away place and recollecting his earlier

59. *anumānam dvividhaṁ svārtham parārtham ceti* ।
— *Tarkasaṁgrahaḥ, Anumānaparicchedaḥ*

experiences, decides that the hill is fiery. This is called *svārthānumāna*. He, then, employs five sub-sentences to apprise another person of this and the same is called *parārthānumāna*.

The five-membered syllogistic discourse (*pañcāvayava-vākya*)[60] is as follows — *parvato vahnimān, dhūmavattvāt, yo yo dhūmavān sa sa vahnimān, yathā mahānasaḥ tathā cāyam, tasmāt tathā* (this mountain is fiery, as it has got smoke, whichever has got smoke is fiery, like a kitchen, this is also like that, therefore it is so).

Just like a group of limbs is called a body (*śarīra*), the group of five sub-sentences is called *parārthānumāna*. As is obvious, none of the five sub-sentences is capable to render the complete unitary meaning of the *parārthānumāna*. Thus the word *avayava* is significant so much so that the *mahā-vākyārtha* of all the five *avāntara-vākyas* is achieved through *vākyaikavākyatā*. *Parārthānumāna* is called Nyāya and the *pañcāvayava-vākya* which proposes the Nyāya is called *nyāyavākyam*.

There is slight difference only in nomenclature of *avayavas* between Nyāya and Vaiśeṣika systems so far as the *parārthānumāna* is concerned. Kaṇāda's *Vaiśeṣikadarśana*[61] proposes the following as *avayavas* — *pratijñā, apadeśa, nidarśana, anusandhāna* and *pratyāmnāya*. Akṣapāda[62] proposed — *pratijñā, hetu, udāharaṇa, upanaya* and *nigamana*.

---

60. *parvato vahnimāniti pratijñā, dhūmavattvāditi hetuḥ, yo yo dhūmavān sa sa vahnimānityudāharaṇam, tathā cāyamityupanayaḥ, tasmāttatheti nigamanam* I — *Tarkasaṁgrahaḥ, Anumānaparicchedaḥ*

61. *avayavāḥ punaḥ pratijñāpadeśanidarśanānusandhānapratyāmnāyāḥ* I — *Praśastapādabhāṣyam*, pṛ.114

62. *pratijñāhetūdāharaṇopanayanigamanānyavayavāḥ* I — *Nyāyasūtram*, 1-1-32

On the other hand, systemists differed in regard to the number of members of *parārthānumāna*[63] — *udāharaṇa* and *nigamana* are the only *avayavas* acceptable to Bauddhas. Either first three or the last three, i.e. *pratijñā, hetu,* and *udāharaṇa* or *udāharaṇa, upanaya* and *nigamana* are considered as *avayavas* by Mīmāṁsakas. A group of Naiyāyikas, Jainas and Bhadrabāhu enumerated the following ten *avayavas*: *pratijñā, pratijñā-vibhakti, hetu, hetu-vibhakti, vipakṣa, vipakṣa-pratiṣedha, dr̥ṣṭānta, śaṅkā, śaṅkā-pratiṣedha* and *nigamana*. Yet another group of Naiyāyikas opine that along with the five *avayavas*, i.e. *pratijñā*, etc. the following five are also essential for a *parārthānumāna*: *jijñāsā, saṁśaya, śakyaprāpti, prayojana* and *saṁśayavyudāsa*.

The semantic/syntactic connection among the *avayavas* is widely discussed in popular works such as *Nyāyabhāṣya, Nyāyamañjarī, Cintāmaṇi*, etc.

Alaṁkāraśāstram

Most of the theories/concepts that are developed/advocated in Alaṁkāraśāstra have their roots in Nyāya, Vyākaraṇa and Mīmāṁsā. The concept of *mahāvākya* is one among them. *Dharma*[64] is taught by Veda like a king's order. Purāṇas (and Itihāsas) impart the same in a friendly manner, whereas *kāvyas*

---

63. *udāharaṇanigamane dvāvevāvayavau iti bauddhāḥ, pratijñāhetūdāharaṇāni udāharaṇopanayanigamanāni vā trīṇyevāvayavā iti mīmāṁsakāḥ, keṣāṁcana naiyāyikānām jainānām bhadrabāhośca mate pratijñā-pratijñāvibhakti-hetu-hetuvibhakti-vipakṣa vipakṣa-pratiṣedha-dr̥ṣṭānta-śaṅkā-śaṅkāpratiṣedha-nigamanākhyāḥ daśāvayavāḥ* । *kecana naiyāyikāstu jijñāsā-saṁśaya-śakyaprāpti-prayojana saṁkhyā-vyudāsākhya-pañcāvayavasahitapratij ñādyavayava samūha eva nyāya iti kathayanti* । — *Nyāyabhāṣyaṭīkā*, 1-1-32

64. *prabhusammito vedaśāstrādiḥ, suhr̥tsammitaḥ purāṇādiḥ, kāvyam kāntāsammitam* । — *Kāvyaprakāśaḥ*, 1-2

explain *dharma* like an affectionate young wife with all kinds of attractions. Any stretch of language ends in *vidhi*[65] (a positive sense suggesting "do this")/*niṣedha* (a negative sense suggesting "refrain from this"). *Mahāvākyam, khaṇḍakāvyam, mahākāvyam, vākyam, prabandhaḥ, śabdaḥ, granthaḥ* are the terms often we come across in Alaṁkāraśāstra — all these are synonyms.

Viśvanātha,[66] the author of *Sāhityadarpaṇa,* defines *mahāvākya* clearly — a group of sentences with mutual expectancy, compatibility and proximity. *Rāmāyaṇa, Mahābhārata, Raghuvaṁśa,* etc. are examples. Depending on the length of *śabda* only the *mahākāvyas* are called *mahāvākyas*. However, "follow Rāma and not Rāvaṇa" etc. can be a *mahāvākya*[67] following the load of meaning, i.e. all the sub-sentences in *Rāmāyaṇa* would have their purport in this sentence. The four *puruṣārthas* or rather eventually *mokṣa* would be the purpose that is going to be served by any *kāvya*. The sub-sentences commending Rāma and condemning Rāvaṇa, are *arthavādas*. On the other hand, according to Śabarasvāmī[68] the condemnation (*nindā*) of a thing/person would have its purport in the commendation of the other thing (praiseworthy).

Ānandavardhana,[69] the architect of the famous *dhvanisiddhānta* (*dhvani* theory), obviously got benefited from

---

65. *vidhiniṣedhāvagatiheturmahāvākyam prabandhaḥ* ।
— *Śṛṅgāraprakāśaḥ*

66. *vākyoccayo mahāvākyam, ākāṅkṣādiyukta eva, yathā rāmāyaṇabhārata-raghuvaṁśādi* । — *Sāhityadarpaṇam*, 2-1

67. *rāmavadvartitavyam na tu rāvaṇādivat* ।

68. *na hi nindā nindyam ninditum prayujyate apitu stutyam stotum* ।
— *Śābarabhāṣyam*, 2-4-2-21

69. *rasabhāvatadābhāsarūpe hi vyaṅgye tadvyañjakeṣu ca yathānirdiṣṭeṣu varṇapadavākyaracanāprabandheṣvavahitamanasaḥ kaveḥ* →

Vyākaraṇa in establishing the theory of *dhvani*, whereas it was from Mīmāṁsā that he adapted the devices like *aṅgāṅgi-bhāva*, etc. in linking various aspects like *rasa, aucitya, alaṁkāra*, etc. He strongly advocates the theory that *rasa* is *aṅgī*, and *vibhāvānubhāva*, etc. *aucitya, sandhisandhyaṅga* and *alaṁkāra*s are the *aṅgas*. Therefore, since the *aṅgas* would be helpful in proposing/stabilizing the *rasa*, the *aṅgī*, there is the relation of principal and subordinate between them. The *varṇana*s (descriptions that are 18 in a *mahākāvya* and less in *khaṇḍakāvya*) are not to be taken as real in all the cases but most of them are flowery/ornamental and useful in the beautification of the *kāvya*.

Bhojarāja[70] in *Śṛṅgāraprakāśa* clearly speaks in support of the *mahā-vākyārtha* of a *kāvya* suggesting the theory of Vaiyākaraṇas.

Vākovākyam is also an example of a *mahāvākya*. A stretch of language, consisting of questions and answers, is called *vākovākya*. Bhojarāja[71] offers the following example. It is a heated argument between husband and wife.

→ *sarvamapūrvam kāvyam sampadyate. . . . prabandhe cāṅgī rasa eka eva upanibadhyamāno 'rthaviśeṣalābham chāyātiśayam ca puṣṇāti* I . . . *yathā rāmāyaṇe yathā vā mahābhārate* I

— *Dhvanyālokaḥ*, 4 *Udyotaḥ*

70. *yastu tadrūparāmāyaṇādiprabandhārthānāmavadhāraṇenopahita-saṁskārasya rāmavadvartitavyam na rāvaṇādivadityā-dividhiniṣedhapratibhāviśeṣa upajāyate sa samastaviśvavyāpī caturvargaikahetuḥ paro mahāvākyaikārtho 'rthamūrtyā vipariṇata-manādinidhanamakhaṇḍam śabdabrahmetyucyate* I

— *Śṛṅgāraprakāśaḥ*, 8 *prakāśaḥ*

71. *bāle ! nātha ! vimuñca mānini ! ruṣam roṣānmayā kim kṛtam?*
khedo 'smāsu, na me 'parādhyati bhavān, sarve 'parādhā mayi !
tatkim rodiṣi gadgadena vacasā? kasyāgrato rudyate?
nanvetanmama? kā tavāsmi? dayitā ! nāsmītyato rudyate !

— *Sarasvatīkaṇṭhābharaṇam, vākovākyam*

Husband	:	Madam !
Wife	:	Hubby !
Husband	:	Please give up the anger?
Wife	:	What have I done with anger?
Husband	:	Weeping because of me?
Wife	:	You won't commit any mistakes that will affect me, all the mistakes are within me (only)?
Husband	:	Then why are you weeping hoarsely?
Wife	:	Before whom am I weeping?
Husband	:	O ! it's quite before me !
Wife	:	What am I to you?
Husband	:	(my) love !
Wife	:	I am not, that's why I am weeping?

Since the whole of the above example has got cohesion throughout, it (*vākovākyam*) has to be considered as a *mahāvākya*. Furthermore, any conversation with cohesion or *ekavākyatā* would fall under this heading.

Therefore, it can be concluded that depending on the *vivakṣā* (a desire to say) of the speaker (writer) either a sentence or a discourse (in most of the cases it is a discourse) is used for expressing the idea/meaning. There will be *ekavākyatā* in both a *vākya* and *mahāvākya*. The words in a sentence correspond to the sub-sentences in a *mahāvākya*.

In Sanskrit it is clear that the deictic elements are much useful in stringing together chunks of language, both at syntactic and semantic levels, into a single unit. The correlatives such as *yādṛśaḥ-tādṛśaḥ*, *yat-tat*, *yathā-tathā*, *yaḥ-saḥ*, *yam-tam*, *yena-tena*, *yasmai-tasmai*, *yasmāt-tasmāt*, *yasya-tasya*, *yasmin-tasmin* (*yattadoḥ nityasambandhāt*, i.e. "which" and "that" are eternally related — is the norm/*nyāya*), *tu*, *yattu*, *yacca*, *yataḥ*, *ataḥ*, *tasmāt*, *ata eva*, *ca*, *tataḥ*, *atha*, *tathāca*, *api*, *apica*, *apitu*, *kintu*, *kiṁca*, *cettarhi*, *na ca*, *kadāpi*, *kathamiticet*, *punaḥ*, *vastutaḥ*, *pare(tu)*, *aparetu*, *itare*, *viśeṣeṇa tu*, *naiva*, *nahi*, *hi*, *evaṁ*, *evamapi*, *iti*, *iti cenna*, etc. are mostly used to denote cohesion among paragraphs or sub-sentences or between the principal and subordinate sentences. Most of these elements are indeclinables (*avyaya*s).

Sūtra, *vārttika*, *kāṇḍa*, *parva*, *āhnika*, *prakaraṇa*, *pāda*, *adhyāya*, etc. are the designations of parts of a large stretch of a linguistic composition built for a single purpose. Here are some terms which are commonly seen across Indian philosophical texts —

Sūtram

alpākṣaramasandigdham sāravadviśvatomukham ।
astobhamanavadyam ca sūtram sūtravido viduḥ ॥
— *Viṣṇudharmottarapurāṇam* 3/5/1

Here in this verse the word *vākyam* has to be supplemented as the qualified/*viśeṣyam*. A sentence (rather an elliptical sentence) — embodying less and less letters, unambiguous, strong enough against any criticism, capable of analysing many an example, not lengthy, impeccable — is designated as *sūtra* (aphorism) by those who know *sūtra*s.

A *pāda*/*prakaraṇam* is a group of *sūtra*s; a group of *prakaraṇa*s is an *āhnika*; a number of *āhnika*s make an *adhyāya*; a *śāstram* consists of some *adhyāya*s.

Vārtikam

uktānuktaduruktānām cintā yatra pravartate ।
tam grantham vārtikam prāhurvārtikajñā manīṣiṇaḥ ॥
— *Viṣṇudharmottara*

Any stretch of language, wherein the things that are said (by the *sūtra*), not said and tersely said are discussed, is called a *vārtika* (amendment) according to scholars in *vārtikas*.

Bhāṣyam

sūtrārtho varṇyate yatra vākyaissūtrānusāribhiḥ ।
svapadāni ca varṇyante bhāṣyam bhāṣyavido viduḥ ॥
— *Viṣṇudharmottara*

Wherein the meaning of a *sūtra* is described with the help of sentences that supplement the *sūtra* and the words of the author of *bhāṣya* are also explained — it is *bhāṣya* according to scholars who know *bhāṣya* (scholium).

Adhikaraṇam

viṣayo viśayaścaiva pūrvapakṣastathottaram ।
prayojanam saṁgatiśca prāñco 'dhikaraṇaṁ viduḥ ॥

An *adhikaraṇa* is five membered — *viṣayaḥ* (subject), *viśayaḥ* (doubt), *pūrvapakṣaḥ* (the first objection part of a discussion) and *uttaram* (*siddhānta* or conclusion), *prayojanam* (purpose) and *saṁgatiḥ* (investigation for further information).

It is across these stretches that we find the frequent use of the deictic elements. Moreover, in the philosophical treatises we come across many an argument and conclusion, wherein the objections already raised in other works and those expected to be made are refuted and the conclusions drawn. In such instances the deixis, either *na ca* (*vācyam*) or *iti cenna* (not to be said/concluded or if said so it is not acceptable) is used. The former is generally seen at the beginning of the sentence denoting objection whereas the latter at the end of the same.

As has already been mentioned, the pairs of *yat* and *tat*, i.e. both declensions and indeclinables have got a relation that is inseparable in Sanskrit literature and this is denoted by the norm *yattadornityasambandhāt*, i.e. (the correlatives) *yat* (which) and *tat* (that) are eternally related. Rather this norm stands as a parameter in establishing the cohesion in a discourse. At times, the latter word of the pair is not employed but supplemented and this is called *adhyāhāra* (guessing). It is just like supplementing a verb, etc. in an elliptical sentence.

Vākyam (Sentence)

According to Pāṇini,[72] the term *vākyam* is a *śabda-saṁjñā* (name/ designation of a *śabda* in contrast to *vācya* which is the name of an *artha*) like *Ṛk*, *Yajus*, etc. Rather he did not offer any definition of his own for the same.

Under *Samarthaḥ Padavidhiḥ* (2-1-1) we come across two definitions of *vākya* offered by Kātyāyana. The first one, i.e. *ākhyātam sāvyayakārąkaviśeṣaṇam vākyam* (a verb with *avyayas*/ *kārakas* and their qualifiers is a *vākya*) is akin to the definition offered by Jaimini, *Amarakośa*, etc. The second one, i.e. *ekatiṅ vākyam*[73] (a group of words having a principal verb is a *vākya*) is exclusively useful for effecting *nighāta*, etc. applications and therefore considered to be a *pāribhāṣikavākyanirvạcana* (a terminological definition of a sentence), i.e. useful in certain grammatical applications.

---

72. *vaco 'śabdasaṁjñāyām* । — *Pāṇini*, 7-3-67

73. *nighātādivyavasthārtham śāstre yatparibhāṣitam* ।
sākāṅkṣāvayavam tena na sarvam tulyalakṣaṇam ॥
— *Vākyapadīyam* 2-3

The founder of *Vākya-śāstra* (Pūrva-Mīmāṁsā), viz. Jaimini[74] had defined a *vākya* thus — if a single thing is proposed/if there is singleness of meaning, and when separated, if the parts therein are found to be wanting, that (group of words) is a sentence.

When it is said that the group of words should render a unitary meaning and must have mutual expectancy or *ākāṅkṣā*, it is implied that *yogyatā* (compatibility) and *āsatti* (proximity) are imperative. For example, "he is watering with fire" is a sentence which lacks compatibility (since fire does not possess the property needed for watering), i.e. although correct syntactically, it fails on semantic front. Similarly, words uttered with long pause in between would not render a unitary meaning and hence, they are to be pronounced in quick succession (*āsatti*).

It is in line with the above argument that the later systemists[75]/commentators defined a sentence as a group of words having *ākāṅkṣā*, *yogyatā* and *āsatti*. *Samabhivyāhāro vākyam*[76] (words pronounced in close proximity are called *vākyam*) — the definition offered by followers of Jaimini also suggests the same.

Avāntara-vākya/khaṇḍa-vākya or sub-sentence is one which can render a unitary sense, but still has got *ākāṅkṣā* that can be put to rest only by another similar *avāntara-vākya/khaṇḍa-vākya*

---

74. *arthaikatvādekam vākyam sākāṅkṣam cedvibhāge syāt* ।
— *Jaiminisūtram*, 2-1-14-46

75. *padasamūho vākyam, ākāṅkṣā yogyatā sannidhiśca vākyārtha-jñānahetuḥ* । — *Tarkasaṁgrahaḥ, Śabdaparicchedaḥ*

76. *samabhivyāhāro vākyam* । — *Mīmāṁsānyāyaprakāśaḥ*

or sub-sentence. Two or more such sentences combine and form into a *mahāvākya*.[77]

A single sentence (which has got *arthaikatva*) proposes a single thing/meaning or serves a single purpose. In such a case it is a defect called *vākyabheda*[78] to split it into two and derive two meanings (*ekoddeśyakaikavidheyakatvam ekavākyatvam*).

Amarasiṁha,[79] the famous lexicographer, had offered the following definition of a *vākya* in *Nāmaliṅgānuśāsana* — a group of *subantas* or a group of *tiṅantas* or a group of *subanta* and *tiṅanta* or a verb with *kāraka*, including *kāraka-viśeṣaṇa* or *kriyā-viśeṣaṇa*, is a *vākya*.

So much so that there can be three types of sentences:

noun and noun	:	*rāmaḥ gataḥ* (Rāma went)
noun and verb	:	*caitraḥ pacati* (Caitra is cooking)
verb and verb	:	*bhavati pacati* (cooking is going on)

Under *Bhūvādayo dhātavaḥ* (1-3-1) Patañjali offers and discusses the last example, which is less known.

Vākyam or sentence is the real unit of language. Even when someone says "door" it is an elliptical sentence — "open" or "close" — either word has to be supplied as ellipsis, as per the context. Similarly, where are you coming from? — "hostel" — "I am coming from" — are the ellipses. When there is shared knowledge and/or wherein the speaker prefers "brevity" —

77. *svārthabodhe samāptānāmaṅgāṅgitvavyapekṣayā* ।
vākyānāmekavākyatvam punassamhatya jāyate ॥
— *Tantravārtikam*, 1-3-13-24

78. *sambhavatyekavākyatve vākyabhedastu neṣyate* ।
— *Ślokavārtikam, Pratyakṣasūtram, śl* 9

79. *suptiṅantacayo vākyam kriyā vā kārakānvitā* ।
— *Amarakośaḥ, Śabdādivargaḥ*

then and there would be an elliptical sentence. Kātyāyana amends — *astirbhavantīparaḥ prathamapuruṣo 'prayujyamāno 'pyasti* (Pāṇini 2-3-1, 2-3-46) — the verb "be" in present tense is there even if it is not employed. Patañjali (2-1-1) says — *vṛkṣaḥ, astīti gamyate* (when someone says "tree," "is" is implied, i.e. "there is a tree"). Elsewhere, Patañjali rules — *na hi padārthaḥ sattām vyabhicarati* (*Tadasya*, 5-2-94) a "thing" devoid of existence cannot be there. It can be presumed that Patañjali made the above statement following *Nirukta*[80] of Yāska, wherein (following Vārṣyāyaṇi) the six stages of a "thing" are described — *ṣaḍ bhāvavikārā iti ha smāha vārṣyāyaṇiḥ* — *jāyate 'sti vardhate vipariṇamate 'pakṣīyate vinaśyati* (born, exists, increases, changes, decays and perishes — these six "stages of a thing" are enumerated by sage Vārṣyāyaṇi, i.e. the same is acceptable to us — Nairuktas). Probably the same might have been a base to the *kṣaṇikavāda* (everything would undergo decay at each moment) of Bauddhas. One can clearly notice the state of "existence" among all the *bhāvavikāra*s. Naiyāyikas hold that there can be a sentence without a verb.

Bhartṛhari at the outset of Vākyakāṇḍa of *Vākyapadīyam*, summarized the definitions of various systemists/*ācārya*s of philosophy:

ākhyātaśabdaḥ saṁghāto jātissamghātavartinī ।
eko 'navayavaḥ śabdaḥ kramo buddhyanusaṁhṛtiḥ ॥
padamādyam pṛthaksarvam padam sākāṅkṣamityapi ।
vākyam prati matirbhinnā bahudhā nyāyavādinām ॥

1. The verb (word that denotes activity is a sentence).
2. The group of words.
3. The *jāti* that is there in the group.

---

80. *jāyate 'sti vardhate vipariṇamate 'pakṣīyate vinaśyati* । — *Niruktam*

4. The partless *śabda* (*sphoṭa*).
5. The sequential words.
6. The assembly of words created in the mind.
7. The first word (of a sentence).
8. Every word (in a sentence) with expectancy.

The sentence is primarily of two types — *sakhaṇḍa* (divisible) and *akhaṇḍa* (indivisible). The *sakhaṇḍa* type has two branches — *abhihitānvayavāda* and *anvitābhidhānavāda*. From the former two sub-branches — the group of words and the sequential words. Bhāṭṭa Mīmāṁsakas and Naiyāyikas follow the said *vāda*.

So far as the *anvitābhidhāna* is concerned, there are three sub-branches — the verb, the first word of a sentence, and each word of the sentence having expectancy. Prābhākara Mīmāṁsakas advocate this theory.

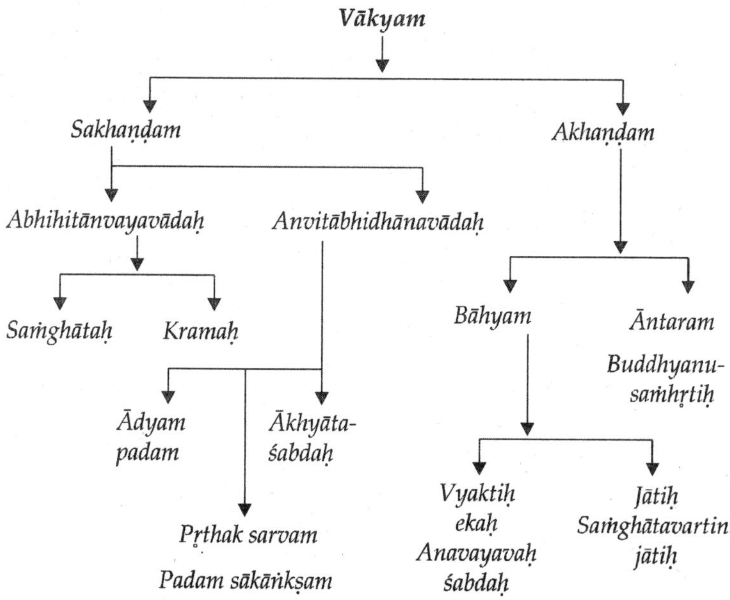

The *akhaṇḍa-vākya-pakṣa* is a synonym of *sphoṭavāda*. Three branches are there in this *vāda* — *sphoṭa* is of two types — *bāhya* and *ābhyantara* (external and internal). *Bāhya* has two sub-branches — *vyakti-sphoṭa* and *jāti-sphoṭa*. Here is a table shown on p. 50.

The followers of *sakhaṇḍa-pakṣa* argue that there are parts such as *varṇa* and *pada* in a *vākya*, i.e. a *vākya* is divisible. Although both *abhihitānvayavādin*s and *anvitābhidhānavādin*s propound this theory there is sharp difference between both of them — *abhihitānām anvayaḥ* — the connection of the meanings expressed — is the derivative meaning of the former. Words render the meanings, and sentence renders the connection among *padārtha*s (word-meanings). *Anvitānām* (of word-meanings already connected with other word-meanings) *abhidhānam* (expression by words) — the words in a *vākya* express meanings that are already connected with meanings of other words, i.e. sentence does not, therefore, render the connections, but renders the specific relations.

The following are the explanations of different definitions of *vākya*:

1. ***Ākhyātaśabdo vākyam***: The verb in the sentence gets connected with *kāraka*s and renders the meaning of the sentence in the form of *vidhi* or *niṣedha*. The rest of the words in the sentence are useful in distinguishing the *vākyārtha* from other *vākyārtha*s. Amarasiṁha says — *kriyā vā kārakānvitā*.
2. ***Padasaṁghāto vākyam***: The sentence denotes the mutual connection of words. A group of such words is the agent of expression.
3. ***Padasaṁghātavartijātiḥ vākyam***: The sequential *varṇa*s in a *vākya* are momentary and hence they are not available simultaneously. Therefore, the sounds

(*dhvanis*) manifest a *śabda* that is different from words like Devadatta, eternal and partless. Such a *śabda* is *sphoṭa* in the form of *jāti*.

4. ***Ekaḥ anavayavaḥ śabdaḥ vākyam***: *Varṇas* and *padas* are unreal. Rather the *śabda* in the form of *sphoṭa*, which is manifested by *dhvanis*, is eternal and single.
5. ***Padakramo vākyam***: The sequence of *varṇas* is *pada* and that of *padas* is *vākya*.
6. ***Buddhyanusaṁhr̥tiḥ vākyam***: The sequence that is perceived at the time of pronunciation is not stable. Therefore a *śabda-tattva* (the noumenon of *śabda*), which is another form of *antarātmā* and which is there in every "being," forms, with false *varṇas* and *padas*, in the mind. The *smaraṇa* or recollection formed due to the *saṁskāra* of such mind, is the eternal and partless sentence. The same is called *vākyam*.
7. ***Ādyapadam vākyam***: Verb or noun, the first word of the sentence is the candidate. Since *kriyā* (verb) and *kāraka* (noun) are inseparable it so happens. The rest of the words are useful in distinguishing the present *vākyārtha* from other *vākyārthas*.
8. ***Pr̥thak padam sarvam sākāṅkṣam vākyam*:** Each of the words in a sentence having expectancy can be considered as *vākya*.

Apart from the above there are a few more definitions of a *vākya* such as — *vidhi* (injunction) is *vākyārtha*, *niyoga* (order/command/employment) is *vākyārtha*, *bhāvanā* (the meaning of a verb) is *vākyārtha*, etc. All of them are different forms of *kriyā* or *ākhyāta-śabda*.

The Kāraka Theory

Having concluded that a verb (pronounced or implied) is the predominant factor in a *vākya*, it is imperative to discuss the structure of a sentence.

The famous *kāraka* theory of Pāṇini is universal in the sense that it is useful in mapping out a sentence, not only the one in Sanskrit but also in other languages, especially the Indian vernaculars. In fact, one would find the grammatical works of all the Indian vernaculars borrowing the "universals in Pāṇini" especially the *kāraka* and it would definitely have a long range influence on areas like machine translation between Indian languages.

When a speaker says *caitraḥ* the listener would put the question *caitraḥ kiṁ karoti*? (what Caitra is doing?) — i.e. there is the need (expectancy/*ākāṅkṣā*) of a verb to render a complete sense. Similarly, if somebody says *āgacchati* (is coming) then the listener asks — *kaḥ āgacchati*? (who is coming?), i.e. the verb needs (*ākāṅkṣā*) a noun to get a complete sense. Such a situation is common to any language.

On the other hand, the word *kāraka* literally means *kartā*. Here the term is used in the sense of "generator" (of a verb). *karotīti kārakam*[81] — says Patañjali. *Kāraka* is a blend of semantics and syntax. *Kārakas* are six. *Sambandha* (relation) is not a *kāraka* for obvious reasons.

The above linguistic phenomenon was closely and keenly observed by Pāṇini and he had earmarked about 114 *sūtras* to explain the same at both semantic and syntactic levels. This theory proves that semantic relations at the word level are fundamental for syntactic structures.

---

81. *kārake* । — *Mahābhāṣyam*, 1-4-23

Guṇaḥ, vṛddhiḥ, varṇaḥ, padam, vākyam, etc. are *śabda-saṁjñās* (names of different types of *śabdas*) and *kartā, apādānam*, etc. are *artha-saṁjñās* (names of different types of meanings) used in Pāṇinīya system.

Kartā

Generally called agent/doer. The one who can act independently is called *kartā*.[82] *Caitraḥ taṇḍulān kāṣṭhaiḥ maitrāya sthālyām pacati* (Caitra is cooking (raw) rice with firewood for Maitra in a pot). In this sentence *taṇḍula* is *karma, kāṣṭha* is *karaṇa*, Maitra is *sampradāna* and *sthālī* is *adhikaraṇa*. When all the *kārakas* are available, the one, who can act and see through the activity is called *kartā*. In the above example, since it is only Caitra who acts and sees through the activity, i.e. cooking, he is called *kartā* and consequently the word denoting him, i.e. Caitra, gets *prathamā-vibhakti* (nominative case). Here the word *caitraḥ* (with *prathamā*) means a person called Caitra, i.e. *prathamā* does not express any meaning other than that of the root (*prātipadika*)[83] here. It may be noted that the word *caitra* in the above example got *prathamā*, as the verb has already expressed *kartā* (active voice/*kartariprayogaḥ*). Rather, if not already expressed then *kartā* is expressed by *tṛtīyā*[84] — *rāmeṇa hato vālī* (Vāli is killed by Rāma) (i.e. passive voice/ *karmaṇiprayogaḥ*). The condition "if not already expressed then only" applies to all *kārakas*.

Karma

It is called object. The thing which is very much desired/

---

82. *svatantraḥ kartā* । — *Pāṇini*, 1-4-54

83. *prātipadikārthaliṅgaparimāṇavacanamātre prathamā* ।
— *Pāṇini*, 2-3-46

84. *anabhihite* । — *Pāṇini*, 2-3-1
kartṛkaraṇayostṛtīyā । — *Pāṇini*, 2-3-18

undesired by *kartā* is called *karma.*[85] *Caitraḥ odanam pacati, maitraḥ viṣam bhuṅte* (Caitra is cooking rice, Maitra is consuming poison) are examples, for the things desired, i.e. *odanam* and *viṣam* are desired by Caitra and Maitra (respectively). When Maitra, fed up with other difficulties, considers consumption of poison less severe — explains Patañjali. *Grāmam gacchan tṛṇam spṛśati caitraḥ* (while heading for village, Caitra touches a blade of grass) — is an example for "things undesired." Touching a blade of grass is "undesired." So the word *tṛṇa* became *karma. Dvitīyā vibhakti* (accusative case)[86] represents *karmakāraka. Odanam, viṣam* and *tṛṇam* are in *dvitīyā.* If there is anything that is not covered by other *kārakas* it also gets *karma* designation.

Karaṇam

The most useful instrument in an activity is *karaṇam.*[87] *Caitraḥ paraśunā chinatti* (Caitra is chopping with an axe). *Paraśu* is the most useful instrument in chopping and it gets *karaṇa-saṁjñā. Tṛtīyā vibhakti* represents *karaṇa-kāraka. Paraśunā* is in *tṛtīyā* (instrumental case).

Sampradānam

The one at the receiving end is *sampradāna.*[88] *Caitraḥ viprāya gām dadāti* (Caitra is donating a cow to a brāhmaṇa). Since *vipra* is at the receiving end it gets *sampradāna-saṁjñā* and consequently *caturthī vibhakti* (dative case).[89]

85. *karturīpsitatamam karma, tathāyuktam cānīpsitam* I — *Pāṇini,* 1-4-49 & 50
86. *karmaṇi dvitīyā* I — *Pāṇini,* 2-3-2
87. *sādhakatamam karaṇam* I — *Pāṇini,* 1-4-42
kartṛkaraṇayostṛtīyā I — *Pāṇini,* 2-3-18
88. *karmaṇā yamabhipraiti sa sampradānam* I — *Pāṇini,* 1-4-32
89. *caturthī sampradāne* I — *Pāṇini,* 2-3-13

Apādānam

Anything that is stable at the time of separation is called *apādāna.*[90] *Vṛkṣāt parṇam patati, dhāvato 'śvāt caitraḥ patati* (leaf is falling from the tree, Caitra is falling from the galloping horse). Since *vṛkṣa* and (galloping) *aśva* are stable at the time of separation of leaf and Caitra they are called *apādāna* and consequently get *pañcamī vibhakti* (ablative case).[91] Here stable means unchanged from the situation/position and not necessarily fast.

Adhikaraṇam

Base, resort or location is called *adhikaraṇa.*[92] *Ghaṭe jalamasti, caitraḥ kaṭe asti, mama mokṣe icchā asti* (there is water in the pot, Caitra is on the mat, I have a desire in salvation). In these examples *ghaṭa, kaṭa* and *mokṣa* are *adhikaraṇas. Saptamī vibhakti* (locative case)[93] represents *adhikaraṇa-kāraka.*

Śeṣaḥ

Literally it means "the remaining" (i.e. other than *kārakas*). Here it is *sambandha* (relation) — *caitrasya gṛham* (Caitra's house). Both these nouns expect (*ākāṅkṣā*) each other (when pronounced singly). On the other hand, the word *caitrasya* does not expect/generate a verb and hence it is not a *kāraka. Sambandha* is represented by *ṣaṣṭhī vibhakti* (possessive case).[94]

Siddhāntakaumudī is useful for a detailed study of *kāraka* theory.

---

90. *dhruvamapāye 'pādānam* । — *Pāṇini,* 1-4-24
91. *apādāne pañcamī* । — *Pāṇini,* 2-3-28
92. *ādhāro 'dhikaraṇam* । — *Pāṇini,* 1-4-45
93. *saptamyadhikaraṇe ca* । — *Pāṇini,* 2-3-36
94. *ṣaṣṭhī śeṣe* । — *Pāṇini,* 2-3-50

Padam (Word)

Earlier to Pāṇini there was fourfold division of words — *nāma* (noun), *ākhyāta* (verb), *upasarga* (prefix) and *nipāta* (pronounced readymade word) — by Śākaṭāyana,[95] etc.). Pāṇini[96] put the entire gamut of *śabda*s under two headings — *subanta* (nouns) and *tiṅanta* (verbs). He included *avyayas* and *nipāta*s in *subanta*s. *Sup* is an abbreviation (*pratyāhāra*) of twenty-one suffixes and all *prātipadika*s (roots of nouns) must have undergone the application of *sup*. In some nouns the *sup* is seen whereas in others — like *avyaya*s it is not to be seen. Whether seen or not once *sup* is applied the root becomes *subanta* for all practical purposes. *Tiṅ* is also an abbreviation of eighteen suffixes. All the *dhātu*s (verbal roots) must have undergone the application of *tiṅ pratyaya*s. Whether seen or not, once *tiṅ* is applied the root (*dhātu*) becomes *tiṅanta*, fit for usage. It was Vārtākṣa[97] and Auḍumbarāyaṇa who refuted the fourfold division of *pada*s.

Interestingly, Naiyāyikas hold that *prakṛti* and *pratyaya* (root and suffix) are called *padam* (probably they must have resorted to the derivative meaning). Meaning is understood through this — *padyate gamyate aneneti padam*. In fact, it was Patañjali who employed the word *padam* in the sense of *prakṛti* and *pratyaya* under *dādhāghvadāp* (1-1-20)[98] and *uraṇ raparaḥ*

---

95. *nāmākhyātopasarganipātāḥ* । — *Vājasaneyaprātiśākhya*, 8-49

96. *suptiṅantam padam* । — *Pāṇini*, 1-4-14

97. *vākyasya buddhau nityatvamarthayogam ca laukikam* ।
dṛṣṭvā catuṣṭvam nāstīti vārtākṣaudumbarāyaṇau ॥
— *Vākyapadīyam*, 2-342

98. *sarve sarvapadādeśā dākṣīputrasya pāṇineḥ* ।
ekadeśavikāre hi nityatvam nopapadyate ॥
— *Mahābhāṣyam*, 1-1-20

padaśabdena na suptiṅantam gṛhyate, apitu kāryam pratipadyamānam pratīyamānam prakṛtipratyayādi tatsarvam padam । — *Pradīpaḥ*

apoddhārapadārthā ye । — *Vākyapadīyam*, 1-24

(1-1-51).[99]

It seems that most of the Vaiyākaraṇas and Naiyāyikas are not aware of their own as well as the others' original concepts of *padam*. Akṣapāda, the author of *Nyāyasūtras*, defines the *pada* as *vibhaktyanta*.[100] This is a different version of *suptiṅantam padam* (1-4-14) of Pāṇini. The Navya-Naiyāyikas (modern logicians) offered a different definition — *śaktam padam*.[101] This apparently extends the jurisdiction to *prakṛti* and *pratyaya*. It may be surprising to note that both the parties vehemently refute each other's arguments, being ignorant of what the original works had advocated — *Mahābhāṣya* suggests that *śaktam padam* has also to be accepted for some reason or the other and the said *Nyāyasūtra* clearly follows the footprints of Pāṇini. In *Jyotiṣaśāstra* also there is *padam* for calculating *kandāyaphala*.[102] In *Vāstuśāstra padam* means plinth area. In Saṅgītaśāstra certain type of song is called *padam*. Therefore, it has to be clearly defined by *ṛṣi*.

On the other hand, a group of *varṇa*s is a *padam*[103] (and that of *pada*s is a *vākyam*). Vyākaraṇam is called *padaśāstram* as it chiefly deals with the form of *pada*. Some Western scholars opined that (Pāṇini's) Vyākaraṇa deals with morphology. In

---

99. *kalpitapadasaṁghātabhakto 'sau notsahate 'vayavasya padāntatām vihantumiti visarjanīyaḥ prāpnoti* । — *Mahābhāṣyam*, 1-1-51

padaśabdena padyate 'nenārtha iti pratyaya ucyate । — *Pradīpaḥ*

100. *te vibhaktyantāḥ padam* । — *Nyāyasūtram*, 2-2-59

101. *śaktam padam* । — *Tarkasaṁgrahaḥ, Śabdaparicchedaḥ*

102. *caitrādititithivāreṣu karaṇam yogakārakam* ।
janmanakṣatrasaṁyuktam tathātristhāpitam padam ॥
— *Nirṇayakaumudī*

103. *kim punaridam padam nāma? kiṃ ca vākyamiti? varṇasamūhaḥ padam, padasamūho vākyam* । — *Nyāyamañjarī*, p. 336

fact, as is seen, it deals with *vākya* and *mahāvākya* also. The topic — whether *varṇa*s are meaningful or not — is extensively discussed in *Mahābhāṣya* by Patañjali. And it is aptly called *śabdānuśāsanam* (not *padānuśāsanam*) by Vaiyākaraṇas.

Padam can be divided into two parts — *prakṛti* and *pratyaya* (or root and suffix). Vyākaraṇa offers *pada*s in both descriptive and prescriptive manners. Through *vidhi*s, the roots and suffixes are offered and assembling them in a right way results in the production of a *padam* — *ram* + *ghañ* + *su* = *Rāmaḥ*, *bhū* + *a* + *ti* = *bhavati*, etc. In some cases the readymade word is pronounced (*nipāta*) and one has to deduce the *prakṛti* and *pratyaya* — *śrotriyaṁśchando 'dhīte* (5-1-84) *śruti* + *ghan* (in the sense — one who recites Veda) *śrotriyaḥ*, *kṣetriyac parakṣetre cikitsyaḥ* (5-1-84) — *kṣetra* + *ghac* (a disease that can be cured in another body, i.e. incurable) *kṣetriyaḥ*. The latter is prevalent in *Atharvaveda*. It can be simply put like this — where parts are offered and *pada* is prepared it is a *vidhi*; where *pada* is offered and parts are deduced, it is a *nipāta*. Literally *nipāta* means pronunciation (of a readymade word).

Some Vaiyākaraṇas (also Śākaṭāyana) and Nairuktas[104] opined that all the nouns are produced from roots of verbs (compare with English — he manned the gate) by adding different *pratyaya*s. This is called *vyutpatti-pakṣa*. Others contest this and advocate the *avyutpatti-pakṣa*. Some ancient (pre-Pāṇiniyan) *ācārya*s[105] like Aukthikya hold that the discussion about *pravṛtti-nimitta*, etc. is unnecessary. The form (*svarūpa*) of a *śabda* is the cause in the expression of meaning. According

104. *sarvam nāma dhātujamāha nirukte, vyākaraṇe śakaṭasya ca tokam* ।
— *Mahābhāṣyam, Uṇādayo bahulam, Pāṇini*, 3-3-1

105. *gaurityeva svarūpādvā gośabdo goṣu vartate* ।
vyutpadyate navā sarvam kaiściccobhayamiṣyate ॥
— *Vākyapadīyam*, 2-175

to *vyutpattivāda*, the *śabda-svarūpa* and *vācya* (meaning), both are the cause and therefore it won't be amiss to offer *vyutpatti*. Although Pāṇini seems to have followed *vyutpatti-pakṣa*, Nāgeśa with all evidence proves in *Śabdenduśekhara* that the former actually advocates *avyutpatti-pakṣa*.

The words are divided into four categories[106] — *jāti* (class), *guṇa* (quality/feature/colour), *kriyā* (action/activity/verb) and *saṁjñā* (name). The word *gauḥ* expresses *gotvajāti* (cowness) and due to inseparability, *vyakti* (individual) is also expressed. In the sentence *śuklā gauḥ* (a white cow) the word *śuklā* denotes a *guṇa*, *gacchati* (going) is a word that denotes an activity. Ḍittha, Ḍabittha, etc. are names. The words in the last category are untranslatable.

The above categorization is done depending on the cause of behaviour (*pravṛtti-nimitta*), i.e. the *jāti*, etc. are the causes in such expression. So far as the *saṁjñā-śabda*s are concerned Vaiyākaraṇas hold that the *svarūpa*[107] (form) of the *śabda* itself is the *pravṛtti-nimitta*.

Like that of *pada*s in a *vākya*[108] the existence of *varṇa*s in a *pada* is also unreal, i.e. *pada* is accepted only for *prakriyā*. In conclusion only *vākya* is the real candidate, as it only expresses meaning.

---

106. *catuṣṭayī śabdānām pravṛttiḥ-jātiśabdāḥ, guṇaśabdāḥ, kriyāśabdāḥ, yadṛcchāśabdāścaturthāḥ* । — *Mahābhāṣyam, Śivasūtram ṛluk*

107. *saṁjñāsvarūpamāśritya nimitte sati laukikī* ।
— *Vākyapadīyam*, 2-366

108. *pade na varṇā vidyante varṇeṣvavayavā na ca* ।
vākyātpadānāmatyantam praviveko na kaścana ॥
— *Vākyapadīyam* 1-73

Varṇaḥ (Phoneme)

According to *Pāṇinīya Śikṣā*[109] there are sixty-three or sixty-four *varṇa*s in Saṁskṛtam (and Prākṛtam). There are eight speech organs[110] in total. It is like a tigress which takes its cubs by clutching between its large teeth without crushing, with fear of falling and cutting that one should pronounce the *varṇas* — says Pāṇini.[111]

According to Mīmāṁsakas[112] articulated *varṇa*s are *śabda*s. They are the real candidates in the expression of meaning. Śabarasvāmī[113] clearly says that the last *varṇa*, coupled with the *saṁskāra* of earlier *varṇa*s is the agent of expression. This is supported by Kumārilabhaṭṭa[114] and Śālikanāthamiśra.[115]

---

109. *triṣaṣṭiḥ catuṣṣaṣṭirvā varṇāḥ sambhavato matāḥ* ।
prākṛte saṁskṛte cā 'pi svayam proktāḥ svayambhuvā ॥
— *Pāṇinīya Pāninīyaśikṣā, ślokaḥ* 3

110. *aṣṭau sthānāni varṇānāmuraḥ kaṇṭhaḥ śirastathā* ।
jihvāmūlam ca dantāśca nāsikoṣṭhau ca tālu ca ॥
— *Pāṇinīya-Śikṣā, ślokaḥ* 13

111. *vyāghrī yathā haretputrān daṁṣṭrābhyām na ca pīḍayet* ।
bhītā patanabhedābhyām tadvadvarṇān prayojayet ॥
— *Pāṇinīya-Śikṣā, ślokaḥ* 25

112. *atha gaurityatra kaḥ śabdaḥ? gakāraukāravisarjanīyāḥ iti bhagavānupavarṣaḥ* । — *Śābarabhāṣyam*, 1-1-1-1

113. *pūrvavarṇajanitasaṁskārasahito 'ntyo varṇaḥ pratyāyakaḥ*
— *Śābarabhāṣyam* 1-1-1-1

114. *samastavarṇavijñānam tadarthajñānakāraṇam* ।
— *Ślokavārtikam, pṛ.* 538

115. *kaḥ śabdo 'bhimataḥ? varṇāḥ, teṣāmeva śrotragrāhyatvāt* ।
— *Prakaraṇapañcikā, pṛ.* 87

varṇeṣveva pratyakṣeṣvarthapratītyupapattaye kaścidviśeṣa āśrayitum yuktaḥ — *Prakaraṇapañcikā, Pramāṇa, pṛ.* 89

Interestingly Naiyāyikas[116] also followed the path of Mīmāṁsakas. They argue that *varṇas*, formed into a *pada* are the candidates that render the meaning.

Aupaniṣadas[117] also feel that *varṇas* grouped into *pada* and *vākya* are the real agents in transformation of meaning.

Vedāntins naturally advocate the theories (in most cases) propounded by Mīmāṁsakas. Śaṅkara,[118] Rāmānuja[119] and some others believe that *varṇas* are *vācakas* (agents that express the meaning) but not *sphoṭa*.

Followers of Sāṁkhya-Darśana,[120] while refuting the *sphoṭa* as unnecessary, oppose the theory of Mīmāṁsakas — *varṇas* are eternal — as unmaintainable.

---

116. *vākyastheṣu khalu varṇeṣūccaratsu prativarṇam tāvacchravaṇam bhavati* । *śrutam varṇamekamanekam vā padabhāvena pratisandhatte* । *pratisandhāya padam vyavasyati* । — *Nyāyabhāṣyam*, 3-2-62

    kim tarhi prātipadikam? kramavadvarṇasamhatirīti brūmaḥ । — *Nyāyalīlāvatī*, *pṛ*. 671

117. *pratyekavarṇānubhavabhāvitabhāvanānicayalabdhajanmasmṛti-darpaṇārūḍhavarṇamālātmanā* . . . . — *Tattvabinduḥ*, *pṛ*. 7

118. *satyapi samastavarṇapratyavamarśe yathā kramānurodhinya eva pipīlikāḥ paṅktibuddhimārohanti evam kramānurodhina eva varṇāḥ padabuddhimārokṣyanti* । *tatra varṇānāmaviśeṣe 'pi kramaviśeṣakṛtā padaviśeṣapratītirna virudhyate* । — *Śāṅkarabhāṣyam*, 1-3-28

119. *śabdasyaikarūpatvamapi na sādhīyaḥ, gakārāderbodhakasyaiva śrotragrāhyatvena śabdatvāt* . . . . — *Śrībhāṣyam*, 1-1-1

    uktaśaktijñānajanyam jñānamāgamaḥ, tatsādhanatvāt varṇātmakaḥ, śabdo 'pyāgama iti gīyate । — *Padārthatattvanirṇayaḥ*, *pṛ*. 50

120. *pratītyapratītibhyām na sphoṭātmakaḥ śabdaḥ, na śabdanityatvam kāryatāpratīteḥ* । — *Sāṁkhyasūtram*, 5-57 & 58

    pratyekavarṇebhyo 'tiriktaṁ kalaśa ityādirūpamakhaṇḍamekam padam sphoṭa iti yogairabhyupagamyate . . . sa śabdo 'prāmāṇikaḥ . . . yena varṇasamudāyenānupūrvīviśiṣṭena so 'bhivyajyate tasyaivārtha-pratyāyakatvamastu kimantargaḍunā ।

    — *Sāṁkhyasūtrabhāṣyam*, 5-57 & 58

→

Pātañjala-*yogins*[121] are the followers of Vaiyākaraṇas. Either *pada-sphoṭa* or *vākya-sphoṭa*, away from *varṇas*, has to be accepted as the agent of expression they hold.

Vaiyākaraṇas[122] have this to say — if it is held that *varṇa*s separately express meaning then each *varṇa* should have some meaning and at the same time the *varṇa*s from the second one onwards would be redundant. On the other hand, a group of *varṇas* also cannot be the agent because of lack of simultaneity (*yaugapadyam*), i.e. all the *varṇa*s are not available at a single point of time as each one of them disappears as soon as it is uttered.

So far as the definition of *śabda* is concerned, Patañjali[123]

---

121. *śabdārthapratyayānāmitaretarādhyāsātsaṅkarastatpravibhāga-samyamātsarva bhūtarutajñānam* । — *Yogasūtram*, 3-17

tadekam padamekabuddhiviṣayamekaprayatnākṣiptamabhāgakrama-varṇam bauddhamantyavarṇapratyayavyāpāropasthāpitam . . . pratīyate । — *Yogasūtram, Vyāsabhāṣyam*, 3-17

arthapratyayo hi varṇairniyatakramatayā parasparamasambhavadbhiḥ aśakyaḥ kartum — *Yogasūtram, Vyāsabhāṣyam*, 3-17

122. *yāvadgakāre vāgvartate na tāvadaukāra iti yenaiva yatnenaiko varṇa uccāryate tenaiva vicchinne tasmin varṇe upasamhṛtya tam yatnamanyam yatnamupādāya dvitīyaḥ prayujyate tathā tṛtīyaḥ tathā caturthaḥ* । — *Mahābhāṣyam*, 1-4-109

śāstrārtha eva varṇānāmarthavattve pradarśitaḥ ।
dhātvādīnām viśuddhānām laukiko 'rtho na vidyate ॥
— *Vākyapadīyam*, 2-210

kṛttaddhitānāmarthaśca kevalānāmalaukikaḥ ।
prāgvibhaktestadantasya tathaivārtho na vidyate ॥
— *Vākyapadīyam*, 2-211

navyanaiyāyikagranthe prakṛtipratyayārthavicārastu vyākaraṇavāsanā-vāsitāntaḥkaraṇatayā tatraiva vāstavatvabhrameṇeti bodhyam ।
— *Laghumañjūṣā, pṛ*. 489

123. *atha gaurityatra kaḥ śabdaḥ? . . . yena sāsnālāṅgūlakakudakhuraviṣāṇinām sampratyayo bhavati sa śabdaḥ* । — *Mahābhāṣyam, Paspaśāhnikam*

and Śabarasvāmī[124] hold extremely divergent views. Through which (illumination of *sphoṭa*) one would get the picture/image of the assembly of different limbs of a cow in the mind, it is called *śabda* (in other words, it is the *sphoṭa* that is the cause and *bauddhārtha* that is envisaged) — concludes Patañjali, whereas Śabarasvāmī holds that the theory propounded by Upavarṣa, i.e. the sequence — *ga-au-ḥ* is *śabda*, rather, the *varṇa*s and nothing else is *śabda*.

However, the Vaiyākaraṇas have the last say — *śabdāt artham pratipadyāmahe* (we get the meaning out of *śabda*) — is the general usage. In case *varṇa* is *śabda* it should have been *śabdebhyaḥ* (out of *śabda*s), i.e. plural and not singular, as one does/cannot get meaning out of a single *varṇa*. Here *śabda* means *sphoṭa*.[125] It is also a fact that through the hearing of *varṇa*s only the meaning is received and not without that (i.e. *anvaya* and *vyatireka* establish the fact that *varṇa*s are the cause

---

124. *atha gaurityatra kaḥ śabdaḥ? gakāraukāravisarjanīyā iti bhagavānupavarṣaḥ* ।
— *Śābarabhāṣyam* 1-1-1-1

kaśśabdo 'bhimataḥ? varṇāḥ teṣameva śrotragrāhyatvāt ।
— *Prakaraṇapañcikā*, *pṛ*. 87

tāvatkālam sthiram cainam kaḥ paścānnāśayiṣyati?
— *Ślokavārtikam*, *Śabdanityatādhikaraṇam*, *pṛ*. 823, *ślōka* 366

125. *evam tarhi sphoṭaḥ śabdaḥ* । *dhvaniḥ śabdaguṇaḥ* । *katham* । *bheryāghātavat* । *tadyathā bheryāghāto bherīmāhatya kaścit viṁśatipadāni gacchati kaścit triṁśat kaściccatvāriṁśat* । *sphoṭaśca tāvāneva bhavati* । *dhvanikṛtā vṛddhiḥ* ।

dhvaniḥ sphoṭaśca śabdānām dhvanistu khalu lakṣyate ।
alpo mahāṁśca keṣāñcidubhayam tatsvabhāvataḥ ॥
— *Mahābhāṣyam*, 1-1-70

anādinidhanam brahma śabdatattvam yadakṣaram ।
vivartate 'rthabhāvena prakriyā jagato yataḥ ॥
— *Vākyapadīyam* 1-1

of *artha*). Rather it is the *sphoṭa* that is suggested by *varṇas*. That is the candidate which renders the meaning. A predecessor of Pāṇini called Sphoṭāyana[126] is believed to be the founder and propagator of this theory which has got its roots in works like *Bhāgavata*.

Medicine, Surgery and Linguistics

In *Caraka-Saṁhitā*,[127] which deals with medicine and *Suśruta-Saṁhitā*,[128] which (chiefly) deals with surgery, 36 and 32 *tantrayukti*s (devices useful in Śāstra) are suggested for unambiguous interpretation and knowledge. In yet another Upaveda, viz. *Arthaśāstra* of Kauṭilya (3-15), a chapter by name *tantrayukti*, wherein 32 *yukti*s are enumerated and illustrated by the author himself, is found. Some deciding factors of meaning such as *saṁyoga*, *viprayoga*, etc. are quoted by the authors of popular Alaṁkāragranthas, like Mammaṭa, Paṇḍitarāja, etc. (from *Vākyapadīya*). These *yukti*s include certain factors already available in Nyāya, Vyākaraṇa, etc. On the other hand, the 36 *yukti*s of Caraka and 40 *yukti*s of

---

126. *vaiyākaraṇanāgeśaḥ sphoṭāyanarṣermatam* ।
pariṣkṛtyoktavāmstena prīyatām parameśvaraḥ ॥
— *Sphoṭavādaḥ, pṛ.* 102

127. *idamanyūnaśabdārtham tantradoṣavivarjitam* ।
ṣaṭtriṁśatā vicitrābhirbhūṣitam tantrayuktibhiḥ ॥
— *Caraka-Saṁhitā, Siddhisthānam*, 40

128. *atrāsām tantrayuktīnām kim prayojanam? ucyate vākyayojanamartha-yojanam ca* । — *Suśruta-Saṁhitā, Uttaratantram*, 65-4
For further details on *tantrayuktis* also refer to

1. *aṣṭāṅgasaṅgrahaḥ, uttaratantraḥ, adhyāyaḥ* 50
2. *carakanyāsaḥ, bhaṭṭāraharicandraḥ*
3. *tantrayuktivicāraḥ, kālameghabhiṣak*
4. *viṣṇudharmottaraḥ, tṛtīyakāṇḍaḥ, ṣaṣṭhādhāyaḥ*

Bhaṭṭāraharicandra are covered by 32 *yukti*s of Suśruta. Here is a brief description.

1. ***Adhikaraṇam***: The main subject of the discussion is called *adhikaraṇa*, for example *rasaṁ doṣam vā* (juice or defect).
2. ***Yogaḥ***: The syntactic connection effected through semantic compatibility of different words in a piece of text or verse, i.e. to put the words in an orderly sentence form, is called *yoga*.
3. ***Padārthaḥ***: The meaning of a word/sentence/*sūtra* depending on *yoga* (above). For example *vedotpattimadhyāyam vyākhyāsyāmaḥ* — "now, we comment on a chapter called the Birth of Veda". Here Veda refers to Āyurveda and not *R̥gveda*, etc. Here by the term *padārtha*,[129] Suśruta means either *vācyārtha* or *lakṣyārtha* or *vyaṅgyārtha*, that can be attained.
4. ***Hetvarthaḥ***: Another sentence becomes useful in explaining the meaning of a particular sentence. For example "clay is moistened by water, similarly a wound is moistened, i.e. becomes septic by (consuming) black gram (*Phaseolus radiatus*), milk, etc." Here the first sentence is useful in explaining the meaning of the second sentence.
5. ***Uddeśaḥ***: A term that is terse is called *uddeśa*. For example *śalyam* — it means an element/phenomenon that generates physical and mental suffering.

---

129. *śaktigrahaṁ vyākaraṇopamānakośāptavākyādvyavahārataśca* ||
vākyasya śeṣādvivr̥tervadanti sānnidhyataḥ siddhapadasya vr̥ddhāḥ ||
— *Nyāyasiddhāntamuktāvalī*, 4

The meaning is understood through Vyākaraṇa, simile, dictionary, statement of a noble man, transaction, ellipses, commentary and supplying a popular word — say elders.

6. ***Nirdeśaḥ***: Descriptive presentation. For example *śārīramāgantukam ceti,* the *śalya* is of two types, physical and mental, i.e. physical suffering and mental suffering.
7. ***Upadeśaḥ***: "One has to follow such and such a norm" — this kind of statement is called *upadeśa*. For example "one should not be awake during night nor should nap during day time." There is slight difference between *upadeśa* and *niyoga*. The former may have exceptions but not the latter. In the present example during summer it is advisable to have a nap during daytime. It is good for a person suffering from phlegm to be awake during night. In the case of *niyoga* "one should take food that is suitable (to his constitution)" means one should never taste an unsuitable dish.
8. ***Apadeśaḥ***: Literally (in Vaiśeṣika also) it means cause. For example "things that are sweet in taste cause increased phlegm."
9. ***Pradeśaḥ***: Application of earlier experience in the present case. For example "this man removed the element causing pain of Devadatta and therefore will remove that of Yajñadatta also." Cakrapāṇi (commentator on Caraka) defined differently — since it is heavily loaded with meaning the subject in question is not fully explained but partly and the same is termed *pradeśa.*
10. ***Atideśaḥ***: To describe the present condition as the cause of future problem. For example "the gas of this man is spreading upward and therefore he is likely to be affected by *udāvarta* (a disease)."
11. ***Apavargaḥ***: Having laid down the restriction generally, if it is made an exception in one or some cases it is called *apavarga.* For example "perspiration

should not be used on people affected with poison except in the case of insect-poison."

12. ***Vākyaśeṣaḥ***: The word needed to complete the meaning of a (an elliptical) sentence. For example "of the head, hands, feet, side, back, stomach and chest" — although it is not stated, it is implied that "of a person."

13. ***Arthāpattiḥ***: The thing that is not expressed in words but implied. For example "I take food," it means he is not interested in rice-gruel. This is one of the *pramāṇa*s (means of knowledge) advocated by Mīmāṁsakas.

14. ***Viparyayaḥ***: Easy understanding of the opposite. For example "weak, having short breath and timid persons are difficult to be treated." It is the same as *pariśeṣanyāya*.

15. ***Prasaṅgaḥ***: Closing the chapter by repeating a statement from another chapter. For example "body is the conglomeration of the five elements, activities take place in such a body and it is the place of treatment" — this is the statement made in the chapter Vedotpatti and the same is repeated at the end of Śārīrādhyāya.

16. ***Ekāntaḥ***: A decisive statement. For example "*trivṛt* is a laxative and *madanaphala* causes vomiting."

17. ***Anekāntaḥ***: Difference of opinion. Some *ācāryas* hold that the *dravya* (substance) is important, others *rasa* (fluid), still others *vīryam* (strength), some others the *vipāka* (digestion) or conversion of food into a state of assimilation.

18. ***Pūrvapakṣaḥ***: A challenging question. For example "how the four kinds of *prameha*s (urinary diseases) caused by *vāta* (gout) become incurable?"

19. ***Nirṇayaḥ***: The response to a *pūrva-pakṣa* is called *nirṇaya*. For example "the irritated air/gas (caused by improper food and habits) initially causes discomfort and then travels downwards and releases urine consisting of flesh-marrow, bone-marrow and fat. Thus the *pramehas* caused by *vāta* become incurable."
20. ***Anumatam***: Literally it means "accepted." If the thesis of another party is not refuted then it is taken for granted that the same is acceptable. For example "there are seven *rasas*" — says another party and since it is not refuted it is presumed that the same is acceptable.
21. ***Vidhānam***: If a subject is dealt with an order/sequence it is *vidhāna*. For example "there are eleven places of fatal importance in the leg." Thus it is described in a sequence and hence the same is called *vidhāna*. Cakrapāṇi says that the *sūtrakāra* having defined/ proposed something, describes the subject and it is called *vidhānam*.
22. ***Anāgatāvekṣaṇam***: To look forward for a discussion that has not been taken up but certainly going to be taken up in future. For example "the author says in Ślokasthāna that this matter will be discussed in Cikitsāsthāna."
23. ***Atikrāntāvekṣaṇam***: Reminding a discussion already taken up earlier. For example "in Cikitsāsthāna the author says, this is discussed in Ślokasthāna."
24. ***Saṁśayaḥ***: Offering reasons/causes for two different things is *saṁśaya*. For example "hitting on *talahṛdaya* (centre of the sole of the foot) would be fatal, whereas chopping off legs or hands would not be fatal."
25. ***Vyākhyānam***: Description in a manner that is different from other Tantra (Śāstra) is called *vyākhyānam*. For

example "*here puruṣa* (person) is described as the twenty-fifth *tattva* (*sūtra* follows Sāṁkhya-Darśana which had enumerated twenty-four *tattvas*). In order to attain *caitanya* or life, Suśruta had taken up the twenty-fifth *tattva*, *puruṣa* (person) and in other *tantras* of Āyurveda (Caraka, etc.) the discussion is initiated (taking the twenty-four *tattvas*) with *bhūta*, etc."

26. ***Svasaṁjñā***: Nomenclature applicable to the Śāstra in question. For example *mithunam* refers to the mixture of honey and ghee. Elsewhere it refers to a "couple."

27. ***Nirvacanam***: A definition. For example "*āyuṣ* (longevity) is therein or people get *āyuṣ* through this and therefore it is called Āyurveda."

28. ***Nidarśanam***: Clarifying an aspect with the help of similarity (also in Vaiśeṣika). For example "the fire coupled with air, becomes increased in sides, similarly the wound develops due to air, bile and phlegm."

29. ***Niyogaḥ***: A norm which says "this only should be done" is *niyoga*. For example "One should consume food that is *pathya*" (*pathya* means suitable to one's constitution). *Pathye sati gadārtasya kimauṣadhaniṣevaṇam* (if one, who is suffering from some disease, takes suitable/restricted food why consumption of medicine?). *Pathye 'sati gadārtasya kimauṣadhaniṣevaṇam* (If one, who is suffering from some disease, does not take suitable/restricted food why consumption of medicine?).

30. ***Samuccayaḥ***: Something that is said in addition. For example "in the chapter on meat — deer, antelope, etc. are important. And *lāva* (?), partridge and spotted antelope also."

31. ***Vikalpaḥ***: Either this or that (in Vyākaraṇa also) — if such a sense is expressed then it is called *vikalpa*. For example "either the juice of meat mixed with ghee or gruel mixed with ghee is good (for health)."

32. ***Ūhyam***: Something that is not stated but guessed or inferred is called *ūhyam*. For example "in *annapānavidhi* (The Law of Eating and Drinking) four kinds of food are mentioned — *bhakṣya* (eaten with mastication), *bhojya* (eaten without mastication), *lehya* (licked) and *pānīya* (drunk). Elsewhere, only two (*bhakṣya* and *peya*) are mentioned and there it is to be guessed that although four types of food is described the popular categories are two only — *anna* and *pāna* (*bhojya* and *peya*). Rather *bhojya*, due to similarity in solid form, includes *bhakṣya* whereas due to similarity in liquid form *peya* includes *lehya*."

2

The Connection of Vyākaraṇam with Philosophy and Sphoṭa

EIGHT things constitute the body of Vyākaraṇa (*aṣṭapadārthīrūpatvād vyākaraṇasya*) — says Helārāja in his commentary on *Vākyapadīya* —

1. *Śabdaḥ*
   1. *Prakṛti* and *pratyaya*
   2. *Pada* and *vākya*
2. *Arthaḥ*
   1. *Prakṛtipratyayārtha* (the meaning of root and suffix)
   2. *Padavākyārtha* (the meaning of word and sentence)
3. *Sambandhaḥ* (relation) between *śabda* and *artha*
   1. *Kārya-kāraṇa-bhāva* (the relation of cause and effect)
   2. *Yogyatā* (capacity to render the meaning)
4. *Prayojanam* (purpose)
   1. *Arthajñāna* (knowledge of meaning)
   2. *Dharma* (leading to *mokṣa*)

Kātyāyana in his first *Vārtika* clarifies that *śabda*, *artha* and the relation between them are eternal and the usage is known through (observation of) day-to-day transaction — then (Vyākaraṇa) Śāstra prescribes *dharma*, i.e. use of *śabda*s (perfect/acceptable to Vyākaraṇa) would fetch *dharma* and that of *apaśabdas* (imperfect ones) would cause (accumulation of) *adharma*. In other words, use and abuse of language is the subject matter of Vyākaraṇa. *Vyākriyante apaśabdebhyaḥ sādhuśabdāḥ pṛthakkriyante anena iti vyākaraṇam* (Vyākaraṇa literally means separation of *sādhu-śabdas* from *apa-śabdas*). Therefore, the term *vyākaraṇam* is pregnant with meaning and hence untranslatable, just like the terms *dharma, puṇya, śabda, dānam*, etc. The word "grammar" is offered as rough translation of "*vyākaraṇam.*" Thus, the form of Sanskrit words is preserved and Sanskrit became the only language that fits computers. On the other hand, since language changes, linguists across the globe have been struggling for the standardization of languages. In order to bring Vyākaraṇa on a par with *darśanas*, i.e. Mīmāṁsā, Vedānta, Yoga, Sāṁkhya, Nyāya and Vaiśeṣika, which are considered to be directly instrumental in the realization of *Brahman* (*brahmasākṣātkāra* or *mokṣa*), Patañjali, in Paspaśā (the introductory part) of his *magnum opus, Mahābhāṣya*, picked up relevant hymns (*Ṛks*) and commented exhaustively. Taking the cue from Patañjali, Bhartṛhari compiled Brahmakāṇḍa (translated into English by Dr Korada Subrahmanyam, 1992) the first part of *Vākyapadīyam*, wherein the philosophical part of Vyākaraṇa is explicated.

It may be noted that in order to obviate the three kinds of defects, i.e. related to *vāk* (speech), *manas* (mind) and *śarīra* (body), of people, Patañjali authored three great works, viz. *Mahābhāṣyam, Yogānuśāsanam* and *Carakam*.

According to Vaiyākaraṇas, the universe is just the exhibited form of *Brahman* (*vivarta* or *pariṇāma* — both these words are used by Bhartṛhari as synonyms in Brahmakāṇḍa — *vivartate 'rthabhāvena, śabdasya pariṇāmo 'yam*; for Vedāntins both are different — if a rope looks like a serpent it is *vivarta*, and if milk turns into curd it is *pariṇāma*). The *Brahman* referred to by Hari here is *śabda* only (also called *śabda-brahman* —

śabdabrahmaṇi niṣṇātaḥ paramabrahmā-dhigacchati — *Mahābhāratam*, Śāntiparva: 232-30, a person well versed in *śabda-brahma* would attain *para-brahma/mokṣa*).

The *vāk/śabda*[1] is considered to be fourfold — *parā, paśyantī, madhyamā* and *vaikharī*. *Parā* is situated at *mūlādhāra* (towards the end of spinal cord) and it can be discerned only by *yogins*. *Paśyantī* is situated at the navel and *yogins* only have *prakṛti* and *pratyaya* (root and suffix) dichotomy at this level. *Madhyamā* or *sphoṭa* is situated in the mind (*hṛdaya*) whereas *vaikharī* is the audible sound produced by speech organs. *Sphoṭa* and *vaikharī* are the subject matter of Vyākaraṇa. Sphoṭāyana, a predecessor or contemporary of Pāṇini is considered to be the propagator of *sphoṭa* theory (*sphoṭāyanarṣermatam* — Nāgeśabhaṭṭa at the end of Sphoṭavāda).

Patañjali[2] in his *Yogānuśāsana* (3-17) says thus — a *yogī* can understand the languages of all birds and animals if he can separate and discern the amalgam of *śabda, artha* and *jñāna* (cognizance). The said trio are identical — *gauḥ* is the *śabda, gauḥ* is the *artha* and *gauḥ* is the *jñāna*. They are there in the mind in the form of an amalgam. That's how an *artha* (a meaning) similar to the *śabda* is understood. *Saraḥ* (lake) does not mean *rasaḥ* (juice).

Artha is of two types — the *vastu* (the real cow) and the *bauddhārtha* (the image of a cow in the mind). Obviously, the latter only is meant in Vyākaraṇa.[3]

---

1. *parā vāṅ mūlacakrasthā paśyantī nābhisaṁsthitā* ।
hṛdisthā madhyamā jñeyā vaikhary kaṇṭhadeśagā ॥
— *Tantraśāstre*

2. *śabdārthapratyayānāmitaretarādhyāsātsaṅkarastatpravibhāga-samyamātsarva bhūtarutajñāna* । — *Yogasūtram*, 3-17
gauriti śabdo gaurityartho gauriti jñānam । — *Vyāsabhāṣyam*, 3-17

3. *ātmā buddhyā sametyārthān mano yuṅte vivakṣayā* ।
— *Pāṇinīya-Śikṣā* →

So far as the *jñāna* is concerned, Śrīharṣa says in *Khaṇḍanakhaṇḍakhādya* that a *śabda* can produce *jñāna*[4] even if the *artha* (both) is entirely absent (*atyantāsatyapi hyarthe jñānaṁ śabdaḥ karoti ca*). *Vandhyāputra* (son of a barren woman), *gaganakusuma* (skyflower), *śaśaviṣāṇam* (rabbit's horn), etc. are examples.

There is a controversy as to whether Bhartr̥hari meant *parāvāk* by his first verse in Brahmakāṇḍa, i.e. *anādinidhanam brahma*, etc. as was commented by Nāgeśabhaṭṭa in *Vaiyākaraṇa-Siddhānta-Laghumañjūṣā*, or he was referring to *paśyantī*, as was interpreted by Somānanda in *Śivadr̥ṣṭi*.[5] Paṇḍit Sūryanārāyaṇa Śukla, a commentator on Brahmakāṇḍa holds that Nāgeśa's commentary is untenable and the latter was under the influence of Tantra. In *Mañjūṣā*, Nāgeśa advocates that *parā* is another form of *binduśakti/śabda-brahma*. The controversy had arisen due to the mentioning of the three types of *śabdas*, i.e. *paśyantī*, *madhyamā* and *vaikharī* only, in Brahmakāṇḍa, by Bhartr̥hari. Nāgeśa,[6] in Udyota in Paspaśā quotes a verse attributed to

→ *buddhau kr̥tvā sarvāśceṣṭāḥ kartā dhīrastanvannītiḥ* ।
śabdenārthān vācyān dr̥ṣṭvā buddhau kuryātpaurvāparye ॥
— *Mahābhāṣyam, Parassannikarṣassaṁhitā*, 1-4-109

vastuto bauddha evārthaḥ śakyaḥ, padamapi bauddham tayorabhedaḥ ।
evam śakyo 'rtho 'pi buddhisattāsamāviṣṭa eva na tu bāhyasattāviṣṭaḥ ॥
— *Laghumañjūṣā, Bauddhārthapratipādanam*

buddhisiddham tu tadasat । — *Nyāyasūtram*, 4-1-50

4. *śabdajñānānupātī vastuśūnyo vikalpaḥ* । — *Yogasūtram*, 1-9
atyantāsatyapi hyarthe jñānam śabdaḥ karoti ca ।
— *Khaṇḍanakhaṇḍakhādyam*
mr̥gatr̥ṣṇāmbhasi snātaḥ śaśaśr̥ṅgadhanurdharaḥ ।
eṣa vandhyāsuto yāti khapuṣpakr̥taśekharaḥ ॥
— *Sureśvarācāryavārtikam*

5. *asatyā yadi paśyantī paśyantī brahma citratā* — *Śivadr̥ṣṭiḥ*, 2-24

6. *svarūpajyotirevāntaḥ parā vāganapāyinī* ।
tasyām dr̥ṣṭasvarūpāyāmadhikāro nivartate ॥
— *Udyotaḥ, Mahābhāṣyam, Paspaśāhnikam*

Hari, along with commentary, and explains that even *yogins* do not have the *prakṛtipratyayavibhāga* in *parāvāk* and hence it is mentioned *trayyā vācaḥ* (of three kinds of *vāk*). A detailed discussion can be had from *Mañjūṣā* and other works. The underlying phenomenon of the Vivartavāda, as per the propagators of Sphoṭavāda is Māyāvāda (of Advaita-Siddhānta). *Śabdotpatti* or the generation of speech sounds is described by Pāṇini in his Śikṣā (*ātmā buddhyā sametyārthān*, etc.)

Why *sphoṭa*? Language is used to transform meaning from the speaker to the listener. Among different units of language, such as *varṇa* (phoneme), *pada* (word) and *vākya* (sentence), which one is the real candidate that carries the meaning — it cannot be a single *varṇa* as the usage of other *varṇa*s will be in vain. On the other hand, a group of them too cannot be, as each *varṇa* vanishes as soon as it is pronounced and therefore all the *varṇa*s are not available simultaneously. Śabarasvāmī holds that the cognizance of the last *varṇa* associated with the impressions (*saṁskāra*) born out of the earlier *varṇa*s would be the agent in the transformation of meaning even if the *varṇa*s vanish. Vaiyākaraṇas refute the above argument as *saṁskāra* would generate a recollection that is relevant to the experience and not the cognizance of meaning also.

Therefore, a candidate called *sphoṭa* is very much required. Since *śabda* and *artha* are identical the term *sphoṭa* is applicable to both *śabda* and *artha* — *sphuṭati arthaḥ asmāditi* (meaning is manifested from this) *sphoṭaḥ śabdaḥ, sphuṭyate* (manifests itself) *iti arthaḥ sphoṭaḥ*.

Literally the term *sphoṭa* means *vācaka* (the expressing agent). It is of eight types — *varṇasphoṭaḥ, padasphoṭaḥ, vākyasphoṭaḥ, akhaṇḍapadasphoṭaḥ akhaṇḍavākyasphoṭaḥ, varṇajātisphoṭaḥ, padajātisphoṭaḥ,* and *vākyajātisphoṭaḥ*. In other words, the first five are *vyakti-sphoṭas* and the last three are *jāti-sphoṭas* (Ref. *Śabdakaustubha* of Bhaṭṭojidīkṣita). Nāgeśabhaṭṭa, and other neo-Vaiyākaraṇas prefer *vākya-sphoṭa* rather than *akhaṇḍa-vākya-sphoṭa* (*tatra vākyasphoṭo mukhyaḥ* — *Laghumañjūṣā*) whereas the Vaiyākaraṇas belonging to the old generation such as Bhaṭṭojidīkṣita prefer *vākya-jāti-sphoṭa*.

Language has to be analysed by Vaiyākaraṇas. But where to start? The actual situation is this — *vākya* (following the length of the meaning to be expressed, it may be a *mahāvākya*/ discourse and hence *mahāvākya-sphoṭa*) is the unit of language, i.e. people employ sentences only, to express the intended meaning. Sometimes, where there is shared meaning or wherein the ellipses can easily be guessed, there it may be an incomplete sentence such as "door" — "open" or "close" as per the situation, "where are you coming from?" "hostel" (i.e. I am coming from hostel). The sentences that are used, being used and going to be used are innumerable. Therefore, the Vaiyākaraṇas had come down to words. Since words are also innumerable, they resorted to *prakṛti* and *pratyaya*.[7] It is just like a mother who employs some pretext or the other, such as cat or tiger, simply to make the child eat the food. Vaiyākaraṇas employed many devices, like *prakṛti-pratyaya-vibhāga*, to finally reach *vākya-sphoṭa*. Due to lack of understanding, Naiyāyikas[8] (logicians) took these (*prakṛti* and *pratyaya*) as real ones and

7. *tatra prativākyam saṁketagrahāsambhavāt tadanvākhyānasya laghūpāyenāśakyatvācca kalpanayā padāni pravibhajya pade prakṛtipratyayabhāgakalpane kalpitābhyāmanvayavyatirekābhyām tattadarthavibhāgam śāstramātraviṣayam parikalpayantismācāryāḥ* ।
— *Laghumañjūṣā, vākye prakṛtipratyayayoḥ kalpitatvam*

8. *navyanaiyāyikagranthe prakṛtipratyayārthavicārastu vyākaraṇavāsanā-vāsitāntaḥkaraṇatayā tatraiva vāstavatvabhrameṇeti bodhyam* ।
— *Laghumañjūṣā, Sphoṭabhedanirūpaṇam*

went on commenting/arguing. Asserts Hari in Brahmakāṇḍa[9] — neither are there any *varṇas* in a *pada* just like there are not any further parts in a *varṇa*. Nor can there be any real difference between a *vākya* and *pada*. And Hari calls it, i.e. the splitting of a *vākya* into *padas* and a *pada* into *prakṛti* and *pratyaya*, *apoddhāra*.[10] *Apoddhāra* is essential for grammatical applications and it may differ from Vaiyākaraṇa to Vaiyākaraṇa.[11] In analysing the word *rāmaḥ*, Pāṇini offered *rāma + su*, Śākaṭāyana — *rāma + ru*, Śākalya — *rāma + ri*. Similarly, for *bhavati* they offered *bhū + a + ti*, *bhū + ati*, *bhava + ti*, so that whatever may be the analysis followed by a grammarian the end-product should be the same.

In the term *varṇa-sphoṭa*,[12] *varṇa* is not a phoneme as it is thought by Naiyāyikas, rather *prakṛti* and *pratyaya* are referred to.

Similarly, the term *jāti* in *vākya-jāti-sphoṭa*, etc. is not the one conceived by Naiyāyikas, rather it is the *Brahman*[13] in

---

9. *pade na varṇā vidyante varṇeṣvavayavā na ca* ।
vākyātpadānāmatyantam praviveko na kaścana ॥
— *Vākyapadīyam* 1-73

10. *apoddhārapadārthā ye ye cārthāḥ sthitalakṣaṇāḥ* ।
— *Vākyapadīyam*, 1-24

11. *yadekam prakriyābhedairbahudhā pravibhajyate* ।
tadvyākaraṇamāgamya parambrahmādhigamyate ॥
— *Vākyapadīyam*, 1-22

12. *tatra śāstraprakriyānirvāhako varṇasphoṭaḥ* । *prakṛtipratyayā stattadarthavācakā iti tadarthaḥ* ।
— *Laghumañjūṣā, Varṇasphoṭasya Prakriyānirvāhakatvam*

13. *yadvā tattadupādhyavacchinnabrahmasattaiva jātiḥ* ।
taduktaṁ hariṇāsambandhibhedātsattaiva bhidyamānā gavādiṣu ।
jātirityucyate tasyām sarve śabdā vyavasthitāḥ ॥

→

Advaitavāda, and Hari elaborates this concept in Brahmakāṇḍa and Padakāṇḍa (*Jātisamuddeśa*). The *siddhānta* (conclusion) is that all the *śabda*s and *artha*s do emanate from *Brahman* only. Brevity has to be sacrificed in case one wants to create innumerable *varṇa*s, *pada*s and *vākya*s.

Vaiyākaraṇas quote *R̥gvedaprātiśākhya* in support of *akhaṇḍa-vākya-sphoṭa* and *sakhaṇḍa-vākya-sphoṭa* — *Padaprakr̥tiḥ Saṁhitā*.[14]

The compound *pada-prakr̥ti*, if taken as *ṣaṣṭhī-tatpuruṣa*, i.e. *padānām prakr̥tiḥ* (a *vākya* is the base of words) then it is *akhaṇḍa-vākya-sphoṭa*. In case the same is taken as *bahuvrīhi*, *padāni prakr̥tiḥ yasyāḥ* (words are the base of which — *vākya*), then it is *sakhaṇḍa-vākya-sphoṭa*.

What is the *śabda* in the case of *gauḥ*? Patañjali at the beginning of *Mahābhāṣya* discusses this question in detail and concludes that by illumination of which the cognizance of dewlap, tail, hump, hoofs and horns is attained that (*sphoṭa*) is the *śabda* (here it is *gauḥ*) — *atha gaurityatra kaḥ śabdaḥ? yenoccāritena śāśnālāṅgūlakakudakhura viṣāṇinām sampratyayo bhavati sa śabdaḥ*. Mīmāṁsakas held that *varṇa*s are the fundamental units. The above question is taken up by

---

→ *tām prātipadikārtham ca dhātvartham ca pracakṣate* ı
sā nityā sā mahānātmā tāmāhustvatalādayaḥ ıı
— *Vākyapadīyam*, 3 jāti-33, 34

evam ca vācyam vācakam ca brahmaiveti dhyeyam ı
— *Sphoṭavādaḥ, Jātisphoṭaḥ*

14. *padaprakr̥tibhāvaśca vr̥ttibhedena varṇyate* ı
padānām saṁhitā yoniḥ saṁhitā vā padāśrayā ıı
— *Vākyapadīyam*, 2-58

ata eva bhāṣye "na lakṣaṇena padakārā anuvartyā" ityādinā "āśitaḥ kartā" ityādau padānāmasatyatvam darśitam ı *satyatve tu lakṣaṇena tadanuvartanamasaṁgatam padaprakr̥tiḥ saṁhitā ityatra tu ṣaṣṭhīsamāsaḥ* ı *tathā ca tatraiva kaiyaṭaḥ — saṁhitaivāpauruṣeyī, padāni tu pauruṣeyāṇi iti* ı — *Laghumañjūṣā, Sphoṭabhedanirūpaṇam*

Śabarasvāmī and the answer is *gakāraukāra-visarjanīyāḥ padam iti bhagavānupavarṣaḥ* (*ga* + *au* + *ḥ* — these three constitute the word — says revered Upavarṣa, i.e. the same is acceptable to us). Therefore, a group of *varṇas* is a *padam* and that of *padas* is a *vākyam* — according to Mīmāṁsakas. In other words, they do not accept *padam* and *vākyam* as something quite different from *varṇas*. Vedāntins always follow in the footsteps of Mīmāṁsakas in such matters. In Taduparyadhikaraṇa in *Śāṅkarabhāṣya on Brahmasūtras*, Śaṅkarācārya, knowing well that Sphoṭavāda follows Advaitavāda, said so — *varṇebhyaścārthapratītessambhavāt sphoṭakalpanānarthikā, yathā kramānurodhinya eva pipīlikāḥ paṅktibuddhimārohanti evam kramānurodhina eva varṇāḥ padabuddhimārokṣyanti* (since the meaning is attained from *varṇas* creation of *sphoṭa* is useless just like ants which follow an order are seen as a row the *varṇas* having an order are seen as a *pada*). In *Śrībhāṣya* under the first *sūtra*, Rāmānuja follows Mīmāṁsakas — *śabdasyaikarūpatvamapi na sādhīyaḥ, gakārāderbodhakasyaiva śrotragrāhyatvena śabdatvāt* (a single form to *śabda* is also not feasible; *ga*, etc. only, which render the meaning, are conceived by the ear and hence they are to be called *śabda*).

Naiyāyikas also accept *varṇa* as the unit. Vātsyāyana explains in *Nyāyabhāṣya* — *vākyastheṣu khalu varṇeṣūccaratsu prativarṇam tāvacchravaṇam bhavati. Srutam varṇamekamanekam vā padabhāvena pratisandhatte. Pratisandhāya padam vyavasyati.* (when the *varṇas* in a *vākya* are being pronounced we hear each *varṇa*, whether it is one or more, the *varṇa* that is heard, gets knitted to become a word, finally the word emerges). Sāṁkhyas also refute *sphoṭa* — *pratītyapratītibhyām na sphoṭātmakaḥ śabdaḥ* (*Sāṁkhyasūtram*) — according to Sphoṭavādins the *varṇas* suggest *sphoṭa* and the same would help in understanding the meaning. This is not acceptable —

when *varṇa*s can render the meaning why another candidate in between? On the other hand, *sphoṭa*, an unknown entity does not have the capacity to exhibit the meaning. This argument is elaborated in *Sāṁkhyasūtrabhāṣyam*.

Followers of Pātañjala-Yoga believe in the existence of *sphoṭa*. Aupaniṣadas (propagators of Upaniṣadic message) believe in *varṇa*s rather than *sphoṭa*. *Tattvabindu*, *Śabdanirṇaya*, etc. are an authority in this regard. By compiling a *sūtra* like — *etena śābdaṁ vyākhyātam* (by *anumāna* itself *śabda-pramāṇa* is taken care of), Kaṇāda, the founder of Vaiśeṣika system made it clear that following *anumāna* only the meaning is understood from *śabda*s (and therefore only two *pramāṇa*s, *pratyakṣa* and *anumāna* are required/acceptable). So the question of *sphoṭa* does not arise at all.

A popular verse in *Pāṇinīya-Śikṣā* reads thus — *ātmā buddhyā sametyārthān mano yuṅte vivakṣayā* [*ātmā* having combined the things with *buddhi* (intellect) puts on the mind with *vivakṣā* (a desire to say)]. Here, *ātmā* is nothing but *Brahman* and the context is generation of *śabda*s (*vaikharydhvani*s).

For Bauddhas and Jainas, everything (*vākya*, *vākyārtha*, etc.) is in the form of *vijñāna* (knowledge). They do not require *sphoṭa*.

The *Dhvani-siddhānta* of Ānandavardhanācārya[15] is totally based on *sphoṭa* theory, wherein it is proposed that the *vaikharīdhvani* suggests the *sphoṭa*. Ānandavardhana and Mammaṭācārya (author of *Kāvyaprakāśa*) had had all the praise

---

15. *prathame hi vidvāṁso vaiyākaraṇāḥ, vyākaraṇamūlatvāt sarvavidyānām, te ca śrūyamāṇeṣu varṇeṣu dhvaniriti vyavaharanti* ।

— *Dhvanyālokaḥ, Prathamānanam*

budhairvaiyākaraṇaiḥ sphoṭarūpavyaṅgyavyañjakasya śabdasya dhvaniriti vyavahāraḥ kṛtaḥ । — *Kāvyaprakāśaḥ*, 1-4

for the "scholars," i.e. Vaiyākaraṇas. Among other Ālaṅkārikas, Bhojarāja towards the end of Aṣṭamaprakāśa (eighth chapter) of *Śṛṅgāraprakāśa,* clearly mentions the *mahāvākya-sphoṭa* that is there in *Rāmāyaṇa, Mahābhārata,* etc.

Somānanda the author of *Śivadṛṣṭi* leads the group of *tāntrika*s in refuting the *sphoṭa* theory, especially the concept proposed by Hari in Brahmakāṇḍa of *Vākyapadīyam.* He was the one who commented on the first verse of Hari, i.e. *anādinidhanam brahma,* etc. as applicable to *paśyantī* rather than *parā* — *asatyā yadi paśyantī paśyantī brahma citratā* (if *paśyantī* is unreal, it is strange to describe it as *Brahman*).

Finally, Vyākaraṇa, Nirukta, Śikṣā, Yoga, Prātiśākhya and Alaṁkāra — are the systems that support the *sphoṭa* theory. Mīmāṁsā (save Maṇḍanamiśra of *Sphoṭasiddhi*), Vedānta, Sāṁkhya, Nyāya, Vaiśeṣika, Jaina, Bauddha, Tantra — are the systems that refute *sphoṭa.* Rather *sphoṭa* is acceptable to Śāstra (i.e. science). It is mentioned in *Ṛgveda* (and *bhāṣya*), *Bhāgavata, Mahābhārata,* etc., works of high authority. The *Ṛk* — *catvāri vākparimitā padāni . . . turīyam vāco manuṣyā vadanti* (four types of *śabda*s . . . the fourth type is used by human beings) — is commented as — *parāpaśyantīmadhyamāvaikharyaḥ* . . . people without Vyākaraṇa-knowledge do not know the other three that are there in the body and use the fourth one, i.e. *vaikharī.* Taking the indeclinable *ca* in *nāmākhyātopasarganipātāśca* of Yāska's *Nirukta,* commentators like Nāgeśa (in Udyota on Paśpaśā) said it indicates the four types of *śabda,* i.e. *parāpaśyantīmadhyamāvaikharyaḥ* and otherwise it does not have any meaning/sense at all. In *Bhāgavata* (12-6-40) *sphoṭa* is clearly stated — *śṛṇoti ya imam sphoṭam supte śrotre ca śūnyadṛk,* etc. Therefore *sphoṭa* is acceptable. The usual behaviour of systemists in Indian philosophy is that they follow the theories of a system irrespective of the fact or personal belief.

Nāgeśabhaṭṭa advocated the relation of *tādātmya* (identity or sameness of *śabda* and *artha*) right from the outset in *Mañjūṣā* (and other works) but in Prātipadikārthavicāra of *Mañjūṣā* remarked thus — *atra granthe yatpūrvaṁ bahuśaḥ tādātmyasya sambandhatvamuktam vakṣyate ca tatparavāsanayeti bodhyam* (it is to be clarified that here in *Mañjūṣā*, the mentioning of identity as relation, earlier at many places and later, is due to the influence of the other system). The other system may be Vedānta as he made this remark while discussing a Vedānta concept/theory and at the outset of the work he quoted *omityekākṣaram brahma* (the single phoneme *oṁ* is *Brahman*). Similarly, Śaṅkarācārya and others refuted *sphoṭa* in accordance with the system they are associated with. Rather they can/do not refute the theory that is there in Veda, *Bhāgavata*, etc.

As has been mentioned at the beginning of this chapter, Vaiyākaraṇas advocate eternity to *śabda*. Jaimini, the author of *Mīmāṁsāsūtras* ruled — *autpattikastu śabdasyārthena sambandhaḥ* (the relation of *śabda* with *artha* is natural) and Śabarasvāmī comments *autpattika iti nityaṁ brūmaḥ* (*autpattika* is a synonym of *nitya*/eternal). Naiyāyikas on the other hand, hold that *śabda* is *anitya* (non-eternal) as the units vanish as soon as they are uttered.

Sphoṭa is described as *nitya-śabda* (eternal *śabda*), *ekaḥ* (a single one) and *vibhuḥ* (pervading). The *dhvanis*, i.e. *vaikharī*, are *vyañjaka* (suggestive) and the *sphoṭa* is *vyaṅgya* (suggested).

Vāgvyāpāraḥ (Speech-Process)

The speaker looks at the *artha* (real or imaginery), recollects the relevant *śabda* and pronounces the same with the help of speech organs (*vaikharī-śabda*). The *śabda* reaches (through the medium of *vāyu*/air) the outer part of the hearer's ear, enters the mind and wakes up the *artha*, that is identical, and the hearer understands the intended meaning. So, the order between *vaktā* (speaker) and *śrotā* (hearer) is *artha-śabda-śabda-artha*. It is also clear that the same amalgam of *śabda, artha* and *jñāna* should be there in the minds of both the speaker and the listener. Otherwise (for example, in the case of a language known to the speaker only) the transaction fails.

Sphoṭa is *śabda* and *dhvani* is *śabda-guṇa* (*Mahābhāṣya*, 1-1-70). It is just like the sound of a drum — one may travel up to 20 ft, another 30, still another 40. *Sphoṭa* is the same, the increase is due to sound (*dhvani*). "We understand meaning from *śabda*, one word, one sentence," (*śabdādartham pratipadyāmahe, ekam padam ekam vākyam*), etc. are experienced by everybody. If *varṇas* do render the meaning then it should have been — "we understand meaning from *śabdas*," (*Śabdebhyaḥ* — plural number to denote many *varṇas*).

3

The Origin and Development of Western Linguistics

THE credit for pioneering the study of Sanskrit, comparative philology and subsequently the Modern Linguistic Theories of West must go to Sir William Jones (1746-94). He (a judge of the High Court at Calcutta (Kolkata) from 1783) founded the Bengal Asiatic Society and delivered eleven anniversary discussions. Jones in fact was the *mārgadarśī* (one who showed the path) to all the Western scholars (European scholars in particular) in their approach to the great wealth of literature related to various systems and sciences that was quite unknown until then. As a scholar of Latin, Greek and other languages he hinted that Sanskrit and ancient languages like Latin and Greek had a common prototype and thus started the study of Indo-European languages. The same, as the time went on, shaped and reshaped itself into Comparative Philology and Modern Linguistics.

On the other hand, before the rise of Modern Linguistics the West had only grammar (of Latin, Greek, etc.), which exclusively deals with different parts of speech, figures of speech and general syntax. Therefore, the West had to coin words for denoting *varṇa*s and aspects and the result was terms like Linguistics, Phonetics, Phonology, Morphology, Syntax, Discourse, Semantics, etc. The interfaces are Psycholinguistics, Neurolinguistics, Sociolinguistics, Anthropological Linguistics, etc.

Rask and Bopp (1814 and 1816) were the scholars who methodically pointed out the relationship among the languages which are the most distant from one another in the Indo-European family and thus began the modern period of linguistics (Holger Pedersen 1931).

Rasmus Kristian Rask (1787–1832) authored a book, viz. *Investigation on the Origin of the Old Norse or Icelandic Language,* which can be called a comprehensive first treatise on comparative Indo-European grammar. Franz Bopp, a German scholar learnt Sanskrit and wrote a book, viz. *Uber das conjugations system der Sanskritsprache,* which treats the verbal inflection of Sanskrit in comparison with Greek, Latin, Persian and Germanic. With its power of stimulation and clarity, Sanskrit had revolutionary effects and it was considered to be "the light from a new Sun from the East."

The Comparative Grammar (1833) of Bopp and *Compendium der vergleichender Grammatik der indo-germanishen Sprachen* (1861-62) of Scheicher were two major works that contributed to the development of comparative linguistics of Indo-European family. Scheicher argued that language is an organism and linguistics has to be considered as one of the natural sciences.

At about 1870 the scenario had had remarkable change — scholars from different nations started working in "Phonetics" in modern languages as well, and "Syntax" was included into comparative linguistics. "Grimm's ideas of the symbolism and sounds" had given a different direction from the hitherto popular theories of Indian grammarians.

Elymologiche Forschungen auf dem Gebiete der indogermanichen Sprachen (1833-36) is a significant work by August Friedrich Pott in phonology of Indo-European linguistics.

Humboldt

For arriving at a reasonable conclusion regarding the analysis of structure of any language it is necessary that one must understand the process of using/understanding the language by a person — i.e. firstly the speaker looks (with eyes/mind) at a worldly thing, gets the idea to speak, recollects the related *śabda*s, conceptualizes the same, puts the *śabda*s in an acceptable order/form and using different speech organs produces some sounds. These sounds reach the listener's ear/ear organs and work up the worldly thing that was already there in the mind and since the listener also has got similar linguistic thinking he understands without delay. This is what is called *bauddhārtha*, the image in the mind.

I can say with all certainity that what Humboldt was referring to by the "inner form of language" was the concept postulated by Vaiyākaraṇas especially Patañjali in Paspaśā of *Mahābhāṣya* — a *śabda* is that by the pronunciation of which one can have the image (or concept) of a thing (mental picture), for example, when the *śabda* "*gauḥ*" is pronounced one would understand it to be a thing consisting of dewlap, tail, hump, hoofs and horns. On the other hand it is the image (concept) of a thing that takes birth at the foremost stage in the mind of any person and then it acquires the form of speech when the speaker wishes to transform such an image (or concept) to others. *Artha* in Vyākaraṇa, etc. refers to *bauddhārtha* (mental image or concept) only.

Rather we find an exact translation of the above concept in his work *On Language* — In itself it is (language is) no product (Ergon), but an activity (Enesgeia). Its true definition can therefore only be a genetic one. For it is the ever-repeated mental labour of making the articulated sound capable of expressing thought.[1]

In philosophy the East had given preference to thought related to internal things — mind, soul, etc. whereas the West mostly preferred to talk/think about things that are external. Similarly in linguistics also as the dictum — "use of *śabda* after the meaning is known" (*artham buddhvā śabdaracanā*) — says it is first the meaning that is important and in accordance with the meaning only the related *śabda* is employed — this is what the Indian linguists feel (*artha* according to them is the qualified, and *śabda* is the qualifier) whereas right from the time of the installation of the Chair for the Philosophy of Induction Sciences at University of Vienna for formalizing the notion of language (not natural language) most of the linguists have been trying to project a theory (hypothesis) that it is the *śabda* that is important and not *artha*. It was, perhaps, after the West came under the influence of Pāṇinian paradigm that the scholars there realized the fact that the semantic front cannot be ignored.

However, still there is another content, viz. cognition (*jñāna*) that is so closely knitted with both *śabda* and *artha* and it is conspicuous by its absence in the works of the Western scholars. In a sentence like "his wishes are skyflowers" — the meaning/thing denoted by skyflowers is missing although one gets the cognition (*jñāna*) out of it.

Perhaps the success of the Oriental (Pāṇiniyan) theories depends upon the above concept. And, in fact the ones which are put forward by Occidental linguists are hypotheses/ conjectures rather than theories. In this context a theory is that which is sustainable and which can withstand the test of time, the Sanskrit equivalent being *siddhānta* — which literally means the conclusion reached towards the end of the arguments

1. *On Language*, p. 49.

and counterarguments (*ante siddhaḥ; vādiprativādibhyām nirṇīto 'rthaḥ siddhānta ityucyate*). For instance the Pāṇiniyan theory is so perfect, impeccable and so strong that the age-old system at which even Śaṅkarācārya expressed surprise (*Śāṅkarabhāṣya* on *Brahmasūtra* 1-3) fits computers of the modern age. One can find analysis of not only a word, but also a sentence and a discourse as well in *Pāṇini*. It's loosely called *pada-śāstra* or in this designation *pada* includes *vākya* and *mahāvākya* as well. Originally Pāṇini, Kātyāyana, Patañjali, Bhartṛhari, etc. prefer the term *śabda* to *pada*. It is *śabdānuśāsanam* or *vyākaraṇam*.

One can find many instances in Humboldt's work (*On Language*) wherein he simply translated the ideas from Indian texts, especially *Śikṣā* (*Pāṇinīya*), *Mahābhāṣya* and *Vākyapadīyam*.

The generation of sounds (*varṇa*s) described by Humboldt[2] is exactly in line with Pāṇini's *Śikṣā*[3] — the articulated sound, the foundation and essence of all speech is extorted by man from his physical organs through an impulse of his soul.

The spiritualistic ideology of Indian grammatical tradition had very much attracted Humboldt.[4] Humboldt believes in line with Bhartṛhari[5] that language, which is imperishable is

---

2. *On Language*, p. 65.

3. *ātmā buddhyā sametyārthān mano yuṅte vivakṣayā* ।
manaḥ kāyāgnimāhanti sa prerayati mārutam ॥
so 'dīrṇo mūrdhnyabhihato vaktramāpadya mārutaḥ ।
varṇān janayate . . . . ॥ — *Pāṇinīya-Śikṣā*, 6 & 9

4. *On Language*, p. 49.

5. *apoddhārastathā vākye padānāmupavarṇyate* । — *Vākyapadīyam*, 2-10
upādāyā 'pi ye heyāstānupāyān pracakṣate । — *Vākyapadīyam*, 2-38
anādinidhanam brahma śabdatattvam yadakṣaram ।
vivartate 'rthabhāvena prakriyā jagato yataḥ ॥
— *Vākyapadīyam*, 1-1

rooted in man's spiritual nature — "already in its first and most indispensable elements, language is so utterly and exclusively rooted in man's spiritual nature. . . ." The artificial split-up of sentences into words and the different parameters employed by different grammarians for this purpose mentioned by Humboldt (the break-up into words and rules is only a dead make-shift of scientific analysis — *On Language*, p. 49) is a clear reflection of the philosophy of Bhartṛhari.

It is interesting to note that the German linguist-cum-philosopher had all the praise for Vyākaraṇa in the following passages — "the Indian grammarians were therefore proceeding with a perfectly correct sense of their language, when they treated all roots as verb roots and assigned each of them to specific conjugations (*On Language*, p. 97); "the combination of the sound-form with the inner laws of language (*pratibhā* and *prayoga*) constitutes the perfection of languages (ibid., p. 88); I shall always take the explanatory examples here from Sanskrit, since this language deals with verbal unity more happily and exhaustively than any other, and also possesses an alphabet more concerned than our own to present the exact utterance that strikes the ear in a graphic fashion to the eye as well" (ibid., p. 111).

It is most likely that the *Langue-Parole* and "Competence-Performance" dichotomy had its origin in the following observation of Humboldt, which in turn had its roots in Bhartṛhari's *Vākyapadīyam*[6] — "the combination of the sound

6. *abhyāsāt pratibhāhetuḥ śabdassarvo 'paraissmṛtaḥ* ।
bālānām ca tiraścām ca yathārthapratipādane ॥
— *Vākyapadīyam*, 2-117

yenārthenābhisambaddhamabhidhānam prayujyate ।
tadarthāpagame tasya prayogo vinivartate ॥
— *Vākyapadīyam*, 2-158

saṁketitaścaturbhedo jātyādirjātirevavā । — *Kāvyaprakāśaḥ*, 2-10

form with the inner laws of language constitutes the perfection of language."

Ferdinand de Saussure (1857–1913) of Switzerland is considered among the pioneers of linguistic studies of the West. In 1959, the Philosophical Library published his best known work (Notes), i.e. *Course in General Linguistics* (*course de linguistique generale*). One is inclined to believe, after going through his writings, that he was not only a philosopher-cum-linguist but also, like Humboldt, digested the philosophy of language of the East, i.e. India. He definitely had the background of Pāṇiniyan system and certainly borrowed ideas from *Mahābhāṣya* and *Vākyapadīya*. The linguistic sign unites not a thing and a name, but a concept and a sound image. The latter is not the material sound, a purely physical thing, but the psychological imprint of the sound, the impression that it makes on our sesnes — this statement has got its roots in *Vākyapadīyam*[7] and other major works like *Kāvyaprakāśa*.[8] Bhartṛhari clearly says that there are two types of *śabdas* — *sphoṭa* (in the mind) and *vaikharī* (the acoustic sound coming out of speech organs). And the sign is nothing but the *saṁketa*

---

7. *dvāvupādānaśabdeṣu śabdau śabdavido viduḥ* ǀ
— *Vākyapadīyam*, 1-44

so 'yamityabhisambandho buddhyā prakramyate yadā ǀ
— *Vākyapadīyam*, 2-40

anuviddhamiva jñānam sarvam śabdena bhāsate ǀ
— *Vākyapadīyam*, 1-123

vyavahārāya niyamaḥ samjñayā samjñini kvacit ǀ
— *Vākyapadīyam*, 2-364

sampratyayārthādbāhyo 'rthaḥ sannasanvā vibhajyate ǀ
— *Vākyapadīyam*, 2-441

8. *sākṣāt saṁketitam yo 'rthamabhidhatte sa vācakaḥ* ǀ
saṁketitaścaturbhedo jātyādirjātireva vā ǁ
— *Kāvyaprakāśaḥ*, 2-7 & 8

(the norm that this meaning has to be rendered by this *śabda*, Naiyāyikas hold that it is the desire of Īśvara whereas others take the *vyavahāra*, i.e. the day-to-day usage by people and it consumes many pages to elaborate this concept). Further, Saussure declares that tradition is the deciding factor in claiming that the sign is arbitrary — because the sign is arbitrary, it follows no law other than that of tradition, and because it is based on tradition, it is arbitrary. The term "sign" as was explained by Saussure (as regards sign, if I am satisfied with it, this is simply because I do not know of any word to replace it, the ordinary language suggesting no other), and in light of its origin referred to above, is fully loaded with meaning. I rather think that the later linguists did not pay adequate attention to this fact and the term is grossly misunderstood besides being misinterpreted, most probably due to lack of knowledge of mental (Indian) linguistic theories. Besides explaining and defining the term "sign" in the said sense, Saussure also declares that in current usage sign designates only a sound-image, a word, for example, "carbon," etc. In order to clear the ambiguity one should do research into various ideas and concepts developed by Saussure and the terms he coined, which are pregnant with meaning. I recommend that the work should be carried out by a scholar with considerable background of Indian linguistic theories and no one else.

The first *Vārtika* of Kātyāyana[9] in *Mahābhāṣya* and the summary offered by Bhartṛhari are taken *in toto* by Saussure while proposing immutability — the signifier, though to all

9. *siddhe śabdārthasambandhe lokato 'rthaprayukte śabdaprayoge śāstreṇa dharmaniyamaḥ* ।   — *Mahābhāṣyam, Paspaśāhnikam*

nityāśśabdārthasambandhāstatrāmnātā maharṣibhiḥ ।
— *Vākyapadīyam*, 1-23

appearances freely chosen with respect to the idea that it represents, is fixed, not free, with respect to the linguistic community that uses it. The masses have no voice in the matter, and the signifier chosen by language could be replaced by no other. The argument that followed the statement under "immutability and mutability" clearly reflects the linguistic concepts of the East that are strewn across various Indian linguistic/philosophical treatises.

The early logicians-cum-linguists of Vienna circle, prominent among them Wittgenstein (1889–1951) held that "in logical syntax the meaning of a 'sign' ought never to play a role." Earlier, Alfred Taraki of Warsaw School of Logicians, had employed some techniques and was successful in the formalization, but without keeping away the meaning. He, in fact, felt that syntax must be supplemented by semantic concepts. Bloomfield and his followers held the opposite view.

Harris (1954 B Paper 8-9) opined that there is no independently known structure of meanings which exactly parallels linguistic structure. At a later stage the harm caused to linguistics by ignoring the importance of semantics (the analysis of meaning) was felt by Western scholars and henceforth they developed the same along with syntax.

As the research in linguistics advanced towards discourse/text analysis, the semantic phenomenon like cohesion/coherence occupied the first place.

It may be observed that semantics in Western linguistics is not as systematic as it is in ancient Indian linguistic study.

Structural Linguistics

The system has got its roots in the *Langue-Parole* concept of Ferdinand de Saussure (1857–1913), the famous Swiss linguist.

The central idea of *Course de Linguistique Generale,* lecture notes published by the students of the scholar, is that "a well defined sub-part of language can be abstracted from the totality of speech." The *Langue* and *Parole* are renamed as "Competence" and "Performance" by Chomsky (probably Saussure, taking into account his Sanskrit grammatical background, meant *pratibhā* and *vyavahāra/prayoga* by *Langue* and *Parole* and this point is discussed elsewhere in this book).

"An abstract system of structural relationship inherent in language and the relationship commonly held by all members of a speech community are represented by *Langue,* whereas *Parole* means the individual act of speaking" — therefore in order to analyse and describe the internal workings of the elements of a language, linguists have offered some approaches and the same are commonly known as structural linguistics.

Structuralism

As it is the case in Pāṇinian linguistics, speech, rather than script (writing) is considered to be the basic element. Speech is primary and essential to script and not vice versa. The linguists during the whole of nineteenth century concentrated on historical linguistics, i.e. to study how the language changes. Ferdinand de Saussure, who is called the father of modern linguistics, revolutionalized the subject by his concepts (see *A Course in General Linguistics — A collection of his lectures*). He wished to treat language as a living phenomenon of studying speech (not written text) of analysing the underlying system of language in order to demonstrate an integrated structure. The well-known doctrines are — *Langue* and *Parole* (language system and the act of speaking) Synchronic and Diachronic, Descriptive and Historical, Paradigmatic (relation) and Syntagmatic and speech and writing.

Langue and *Parole* were referred to as Competence and Performance by later linguists (Chomsky, etc). The different relationships between the units of language, such as words are referred to by the terms paradigmatic and syntagmatic. According to occidental linguists, a sentence or phrase or word is nothing but a sequence of signs. Each sign, according to them, contributes to the meaning of the whole unit. The sequence described above is called syntagmatic (or horizontal) relationship between the signs. In other words, all the words in a sentence must be related to each other and then only that particular group of words can be called a sentence (compare with *ākāṅkṣā* and the group of words such as *gauḥ, aśvaḥ, puruṣaḥ, hastī, brāhmaṇaḥ* — which cannot be called a sentence). Occidental theorists rule that phonemes are meaningless (see Pratyāhārāhnika of *Mahābhāṣya*: *kimarthavanto varṇāḥ*). Syntagmatic and horizontal are synonyms. Such relationship between signs forms structure. Therefore, a particular order of signs/units/sounds (E.g. *r* + *a* + *t* for a word and He will go tomorrow = pro + aux + main verb + Adv. — for a sentence) is called sequence.

Similarly, at the level of a word/phrase/sentence, there will be paradigmatic relationship between a sign inside the structure and the one outside. The word "he" in the sentence "He will go tomorrow" has got paradigmatic relationship with It/They/We/She, etc. which are outside the structure and belong to the same (pronoun) system (group). So the relationship here is vertical. According to J.R. Firth, structures are horizontal and systems are vertical and the first principle of linguistic analysis is to distinguish between structures and systems.

Among the American linguists it was Edward Sapir and Leonard Bloomfield who followed in the footsteps of Saussure and started working on structural linguistics. Sapir published papers on the *Functioning of Language in Creative Literature, Mythology and Religion.*

Language (1933) of Bloomfield had considerably influenced the American linguistics and the book, apart from published papers based on fieldwork, had a good impact. He was initially a mentalist but later became an empiricist — he believed, statements concerning linguistics should be made after "direct observation of the phenomena" or generalizations that could be drawn from observables by a set of mechanical procedures. In spite of the fact that he studied Sanskrit and recognized it as a fertile source for various aspects of language, Bloomfield advocated the study of language without recourse to meaning, which is quite opposite to the theory of Sanskrit grammarians like Kātyāyana and Patañjali, i.e. the *śabda, artha* and their relation are eternal (*siddhe śabdārthasambandhe* — Paspaśāhnika of *Mahābhāṣya*).

It was during and after the war that the empiricist outlook of Bloomfield and his followers predominated the mentalistic approach of Sapir and his students. Similarly, during 1945 and 1955 American structural linguists, who were vehemently trying to bring linguistics on a par with natural sciences, had prospered at the cost of their European counterparts, who were more concerned about the philosophy underlying the nature of language. On the other hand, there was a clear watershed between European and American linguists with regard to "meaning." The former, probably due to the strong influence of Sanskrit linguistics, felt that "meaning" that is primarily conveyed by language (and cannot be separated from language as well) should be coupled with the study of language, whereas the latter equally strongly felt that "meaning" and its study are a mere waste! The post-

Bloomfieldian linguists started to discover a grammar, which can describe the speech in the following order:

1. Phonemics (Phonology)
2. Morphemics (Morphology)
3. Syntax
4. Semantics

Later linguists (*Amesterdam Studies . . . Current Issues*, vol. I, p. 303) bluntly refuted the claims of expounders and propagators of "Generative Grammar" — in sum, a transformational generative grammar is incapable in principle of serving as an idealized model of linguistic performance because it lacks certain requisite properties which any model of this sort must possess. In fact, under a dynamic interpretation of the sort suggested, a generative grammar won't seem capable of serving only as a model of random sentence production, being inherently incapable (because of its unidirectional character) of serving as a model of speech perception of any sort. From this we can conclude that there is no apparent substance to Chomsky's claim that a generative grammar describes and attempts to account for the ability of a speaker to understand an arbitrary sentence of his language and to produce an appropriate sentence on a given occasion (1966b: 3), nor to the implication that the rules which appear in such grammars determine how sentences are to be formed, used and understood (Chomsky 1965: 25).

The downfall of post-Bloomfieldian linguistics was hastened by dramatic changes of outlook in the philosophy of science (Newmeyer 1986). Therefore there was a crisis in empirical philosophy towards later 1950s and empiricism was evidently on decline.

Discovery of Sanskrit and the Revolution in the Western World

The credit of revolutionizing the so-called modern linguistics should go to the ancient and perfect language from the Indian subcontinent, Sanskrit. A renowned Western scholar, Holger Paderson summed up the then prevailing situation — The knowledge of Sanskrit was found to have revolutionary consequences. The mere fact that scholars were unexpectedly confronted with a third classical language, in addition to Greek and Latin, was sufficient to shake their reliance on the easy-going ways of thinking that had satisfied previous centuries. Latin had been regarded as a sort of corrupted Greek and the resemblances between Latin and the other European languages had been explained in the superficial way as due to the prepondering cultural influence of Latin in Europe. But a similar off hand explanation of the resemblances between the ancient languages and this new-found Sanskrit was not possible; its home was too distant and its remote cultural world was entirely independent of both Greco-Roman and modern civilization.

Refutations-Within

While Van Dijk and others refer to "pragmatic rules" one must not be misled into thinking that such rules are highly formalized within an aximatized system like the rules of generative grammar. In cases they tend to be fragmentary or isolated and used rather loosely, i.e. in the way that Labov (1972b) refers to "rules for ritual insults" such "rules" better be turned "statements," "conditions," "principles," "maxims," "strategies" and so on, rather than rules. And to be sure, such terms have often been employed (cf. Grice's 1975 maxims, Gumpherz's 1982a "strategies" and Series 1969, 1979 "conditions").

Phonology

It deals with the sorts of sound used in speech and how they are produced and detected. Phonemics is the old term. A phoneme does not have any meaning (compare with the *varṇa* — alphabet in *Pāṇini*).

Phonetics or articulatory phonetics is concerned with the sounds, which occur in language in general (and therefore not phonemic status) as articulatory and acoustic events. There can be distinct sounds (called allophones) of the same phoneme in a particular language.

The organs of speech (compare with *Pāṇinīya-Śikṣā — aṣṭau sthānāni varṇānām*; i.e. eight places wherein phonemes are produced, etc.) according to modern linguists (Hockett 1976) "consist of all the movable parts in the oral cavity (mouth), the nasal cavity, the pharynx (throat) and the lungs, together with the muscles that move these parts." Collectively this region is called speech tract.

Morphology

Morphemics is the old term. Morphemes are the smallest individually meaningful elements (compare with *prakṛti* and *pratyaya* in *Pāṇini*). In other words, the analysis/construction of a word is called Morphology. In the word "younger" there are two morphemes and so on. There are many definitions of a "word" but none of them is exhaustive (compare with *suptiṅantam padam* of *Pāṇini*). Morpheme is the minimal unit of grammatical analysis (Lyon). Lyon and Aitchison think that morpheme is a grammatical unit rather than a meaningful unit. According to Bloomfield word is a "minimum free form." Another definition is — a word may be defined as the union of a particular meaning with a particular complex of sounds capable of a particular grammatical employment. To quote

Palmer, "in conclusion, sadly, we have to say that the word is not a clearly definable linguistic unit . . . what the word is or is not, depends ultimately on our TOTAL view of grammar." All words are morphemes but all morphemes are not words. There will be two kinds of morphemes — free and bound, also known as root/base/stem and affix (compare with *dhātu/ prātipadikam* and *pratyaya* of *Pāṇini*).

The ways in which the morphemes of a given language are variously represented by phonemic shapes can be regarded as a kind of code — and this is called morphophonemics.

A morpheme is represented by one phoneme or sometimes by more than one. Each representation is a morph; all the morphs which represent some given morpheme are called allomorphs of the morpheme. Thus/sil/and/s . . . l/ are both allomorphs of the morpheme {sell}.

Grammar and morphophonemics are separate sub-systems of a language, but grammatical and morphophonemic analyses necessarily proceed hand in hand.

Syntax

Syntax includes the ways in which words and suprasegmental morphemes are arranged relative to each other in utterances. A morpheme which occurs only as part of all of some word is a segmental morpheme : John, treat; — s. A morpheme which is not part of a word is suprasegmental : all intonations, and some other morphemes such as the secondary stress / ̀ / on the second segmental constituent of */mǽč+bàks/* (matchbox — Hocket, *A Course in Modern Linguistics* p. 168), which is not part of the word "box." The line of demarcation between morphology and syntax is not so clear-cut always. Where morphology ends, syntax starts.

A sentence is a grammatical form which is not in construction with any other grammatical form: a constitute which is not a constituent (compare with *arthaikatvādekam vākyam* of *Jaimini*).

Syn-taxis (Greek) means placing/putting together (compare with *samabhivyāhāro vākyam* — juxtaposition (of words) is sentence — of *Mīmāṁsāparibhāṣā*).

The immediate constituents of "Poor John ran away" are the two forms — "Poor John" and "ran away" (Bloomfield, *Language*). Immediate constituent analysis (ICs for short) is a technique useful in the analysis of a sentence — the parts therein and their relationship.

Discourse

Any stretch of language beyond a sentence with textual unity (cohesion and coherence) as the underlying fundamental phenomenon is a discourse. Aristotle defines a rhetoric (the study of discourse) thus — rhetoric is the theory and practice of persuasion by means of reasoned discourse. Aristotle's consideration of ordered piece of rhetoric is thus introduction, statement, argument and epilogue. Plato states — discourse ought to be considered like a living creature with its own body, as it were; it must not lack either head or feet, it must have a middle and extremities so composed as to suit each other and the whole work (according to his opinion all discourse is rhetorical and conforms to the norms of rhetoric). Halliday, Hasan (1976), Van Dijk (1977), Hobbs (1978-79), etc. are prominent among those who worked on this aspect in modern times.

Zellig Harris opined that "language does not occur in stray words or sentences but in connected discourse — from a monologue to a union square argument and whether it be a paragraph or a book." He also elaborated — it is nothing but a string of linguistic forms arranged in successive sentences. There we can find relative occurrence of these elements with respect to each other.

In Russian linguistics too, I.A. Figuroviskij, through numerous examples, had shown that in teaching language it is necessary to teach the structure of the paragraph, completely in the same manner as the structures of words and sentences are taught.

Pieter A.M. Seuren in his work *Discourse Semantics* (p. 20) confesses that "(because) discourse theory is still an unknown entity."

Elinor Ochs and Bamgi B. Schieffalin (*Subject and Topic*, p. 340) in their article on "Topic as a Discourse Notion" tried to elaborate the concept of Discourse from Western linguistic viewpoint — any sequence of two or more utterances produced by a single speaker or by two or more speakers who are interacting with one another (at some point in time and space). Discourses may evolve or develop in several ways.

For example, a stretch of discourse may contain a series of linked discourse topics. The discourse topics are linked in the sense that the propositional content is drawn from one or more of the utterances already produced in the discourse. Blakemore (*Cambridge Survey* IV, p. 231) summarizes the statements of some of the linguists with regard to discourse — Halliday and Hasan (1976), Van Dijk (1977) and Hobbs (1978-79), who were analysing a discourse felt that textual unity or coherence is the underlying fundamental phenomenon of a discourse. Halliday and Hasan consider that the cohesion in a text (discourse) is maintained through pronouns like "his" and "her" as well as the temporal terms like "then" and "now," and the words like "so" and "that's why." Halliday and Hasan consider a text to be a unit of language rather than a set of sentences but add that the meaning relations are realized by sentences.

Deictic Elements

Deictic elements are words (including prepositional phrases) which are useful in connecting sub-sentences in a discourse. The semantic relations of different sub-sentences and paragraphs are maintained by these paradigms and thus the cohesion across the entire discourse is secured.

John Lyons feels that "deixis" is like reference, with which it overlaps, in that it relates to their context of occurrence. Reference can be either deictic or non-deictic and deixis does not necessarily involve reference. The essential property of deixis (the term comes from the Greek word meaning "pointing" or "showing") is that it determines the structure and interpretation of utterances in relation to the time and place of their occurrence, the identity of the speaker and the addressee, and objects and events in the actual situation of the utterance. For example, the referrent of "that man over there" cannot be identified except in relation to the use of the expression by someone who is in a particular place on a particular occasion.

In the book *Words, Meanings and Messages* the author says thus about the deictic signs — the most immediately transparent articulation between the act of speech and its behavioural setting is found in conjunction with components of linguistic media, which are called deictic signs. Deictic signs are signs or components of sign compounds which involve a reference to the act of speech in which they are involved. Wein Reich wrote about these signs as follows — among the factors of the speech situation, which are utilized in deixis are the following : the utterer of the discourse (1st person) or the receiver (2nd person), the time of discourse (tense) and its place (varieties of demonstration) and the identity or the non-identity of the act of discourse (anaphora, reflexiveness, obviation, etc.)

That this paradigm constitutes a striking universal of language can be appreciated not only from its widespread distribution, but also visualizing further factors of speech situation, which could be but do not seem to be, utilized in any language; the loudness of speech, its speed, the certainty of the assertion. No language seems to have adverbs meaning — "louder than I am now speaking," "as slow as my speech now" and the like.

In their book *Introduction to Text Linguistics* the authors (translators) say the following about conjunctions — conjunction can link utterances not formatted as complete sentences at all: provided an addictive or interdependent relationship obtains. Conjunction is the default junction, since, unless specified otherwise, events and situations combined addictively in a textual world. There is a motive to place "and," "also," "in addition," etc. between all clauses or sentences; in fact, such a practice renders the text dull, except for occasional special effects (of the device of "polysyndeton" in classical rhetoric). The use of such junctions is more likely when interdependency is not obvious and should be stressed. Disjunction is nearly always signalled by "or" (sometimes expanded to "either or"; "whether or not," etc.); it is most commonly employed within sentences.

There are a good number of deictic elements in English language which are mostly useful in maintaining the cohesion —

1. *Reference*	
(a) *Pronominals*	he, him, his, she, her, hers, it, its, they, their, theirs
(b) *Demonstrative*	this/these, that/those, Definite Article — here/there, the
(c) *Comparatives*	some, identical, similar, such, different, other, else, more, less, as many
2. *Substitution*	
Nominal	one/ones, the same, so
Verbal	be, have, do, do so, be so, likewise, be it/that, do it/that
Clausal	so, not
3. *Ellipsis*	Nominal, Verbal and Clausal ellipses
4. *Conjunction*	
Addition	and, and also, not, and . . . not, or, or else, furthermore, alternatively, by the way, incidentally, that is, in other words, for example, thus, likewise, in the same way, on the other hand, by contrast
Adversative	yet, though, only, but, however, even so, all the same, in fact, actually, conversely, on the other hand, instead, on the contrary, rather, at least, I mean, or rather, in any case, anyhow

Casual	so, then, therefore, consequently, on account of this, in consequence with this in mind, for, because, it follows to this end, arising out of this, then, in that case, in such an event, under the circumstances, in this respect, here, apart from this, in other respects
Temporal	then, next, just, then before that, hitherto, in the end, finally, in conclusion, first . . . then, at first, originally, formerly . . . now, at once, soon, next time/day, meanwhile, until/then, at this moment, up to now, at this point, from now on, to sum up, to conclude with, to resume
Others	now, of course, well, surely, after all, any way
5. *Lexical*	Same item, synonym or near synonym, collocation, etc.

Machine Translation

Translation through computer machines has been going on for decades at a number of places across the globe. Morphological analysers are used for this purpose generally. The fact one should note is that since the machine does not possess "intellect" (*buddhi*) it cannot think like a human being (see the discussion on *pratibhā* in this book). If one can inject or insert *buddhi* into the machine then it would be possible to have some meaningful result. Otherwise it would be "garbage in" — "garbage out" — as usual. I experimented with Telugu and Hindi.

In 1949 a memorandum submitted by Warren Weaver proposed the idea of machine translation, i.e. translation by computers, for the first time. By 1955, such translation work was going on in three countries at half a dozen institutions. Linguists also had an idea of using computers for linguistic analysis.

After Second World War the globe was divided into Eastern Communistic Block and Western Democratic Block. The then USSR was leading the former, whereas USA was taking care of the latter. Cold war, apart from expionage and counter-expionage, was rampant between the super powers. It is believed that Russians had succeeded in inventing a computer system that can be used for translation exclusively in the field of defence. "Information Theory" — a new field proposed by Shanon and Weaver (1949) — promised the usefulness of study of the statistical structure of language (especially English) which will also be significant to students of language and communication.

It was probably against this background that Noam Chomsky published *Syntactic Structures* (early 1957) introducing Transformational Generative Grammar (TGG). The author advocated grammar as a theory of language. The book demonstrates "the practical possibility of a non-empiricist theory of linguistic structure." Four external conditions of adequacy are outlined in syntactic structures, which can be a way of evaluation of grammars —

1. The sentences generated are acceptable to the native speaker.
2. Every case of a "constitutional homonymity" (the assignment of more than one structural description to a sentence) describes a real ambiguity, and every case of ambiguity is represented by constructional homonymity.

3. Differential interpretations of superficially similar sentences are represented by different derivational histories.
4. Sentences understood in similar ways are represented in similar ways at one level of description.

Chomsky refuted both Finite State Grammar and Phrase structure Grammar as inadequate in terms of generative capacity. He felt that in order to formalize the linguistic theory a generative grammar coupled with phrase structure rules is necessary. And the model he envisaged had three levels — phrase structure, transformational structure and morphophonemics. I think that we are forced to conclude that grammar is autonomous and independent of meaning (p. 17) — such statements clearly show that he followed the path of the post-Bloomfieldian structuralists like Harris and Bloch so far as the role of meaning is concerned (compare this approach with Kāraka Theory of Pāṇini where the underlying semantic relations are much more important in deciding the structure of a sentence and this may have a universal application).

Simultaneously there was considerable work done on generative phonology, wherein we find three trends, i.e. the phonological processes of Sapir et al., process of the formalization of rules of post-Bloomfieldians; and the phonological theory of Prague School (contributed by Prince N.S. Trubetskoi, etc.). Morris Halle and Chomsky along with Fred Lukoff worked on accent and juncture in English. The rules and arguments are analogous to the pattern common in Sanskrit vowel *sandhi*.

It was in 1963 that two philosophers, Jerrow Katz and Jerry Fodor, had developed a theory of transformational generative grammar wherein semantics was incorporated. Katz and Fodor concluded that a line had to be drawn between those aspects of sentence interpretation deriving from linguistic knowledge and those deriving from beliefs about the world (Newmeyer 1986).

In 1964 Chomsky coined two terms (almost in line with Saussure's *Langue* and *parole*) "Competence" and "Performance" (1964b : 915). The innate grammatical knowledge of a person (*pratibhā* — Bhartṛhari) is Competence whereas the actual use of language (*vyavahāra* or *prayoga* or *abhidhāna*) is Performance.

Substantive universals and formal universals are proposed by Katz and Postal (1964) and Chomsky (1965). Syntactic categories, semantic markers, etc. fall under the former, whereas the formal conditions of grammatical description are dealt with by the latter.

In 1965 Chomsky published another book — *Aspects of the Theory of Syntax* — in which he replaced generalized transformations with phrase structure and separated sub-categorization and lexical rules from phrase structure rules. The "inner form" of Wilhelm von Humboldt (1836) was replaced by the term "deep structure" and it is defined by phrase structure rules, sub-categorization rules (base rules) and rules of lexical insertion. Being a post-Bloomfieldian, in this work also, Chomsky separated syntax from semantics. He rather got confused.

However, there were linguists like Kuroda (1972) who recognized that the sounds represent the meaning and this should be the basis for generative semantics.

In late 1960s, Charless Fillmore, proposed "Case Grammar" after refuting aspects model. According to this theory, apart from a verb, a sentence consists of an unordered series of semantically characterizable thematic roles or cases.

The similarity between generative semantics and case grammar was that both proposed meaning as the base for syntactic structure.

Gradually the importance of meaning was realized more and more by linguists like Ray Jackendoff (*Semantic Interpretation in Generative Grammar* — 1972) and semantics was the major thrust of linguistic study during 1970s. The following are the four postulates of Jackendoff useful for semantic interpretation (reproduced from Newmeyer 1986) —

1. ***Functional Structure***: The main propositional content of the sentence (essentially, the semantic relationship between a verb and its noun phrase, co-constituents within a clause).
2. ***Modal Structure***: The specification of the scope of logical elements, such as negation and quantifiers, and of the referential properties of noun phrase.
3. ***The table of reference***: The specification of which noun phrases in a sentence are understood as co-referential.
4. ***Focus and Presupposition***: The designation of what information in the sentence is understood as new and what is understood as old.

X-bar Theory

The theory is also a part of the English grammar and was first proposed by Chomsky (Remarks on "Normalization" 1970) for the purpose of regulating the structure of phrases. According to this theory all phrases are headed by a lexical head, i.e. all phrases are "endocentric." The lexical head of the projection is a zero projection (X^0), X-bar theory distinguishes two levels of projection. Complements combine with X to form X^1 projections (*c* below); adjuncts combine with X^1 to form X^1 projections (*b*). The specifier combines with the topmost X^1 to form the maximal projection X^{11} (*a*). For convenience sake we replace X^{11} by *P*

a X^{11} ———> Spec; X^1

b X^{1*} ———> *X; YP*

c X^1 ———> *X; YP*

Government Binding Theory

Government Binding Theory is a development of earlier versions of generative grammar initiated by Noam Chomsky. In the framework of generative syntax the constituent structure of a sentence is represented in one of the following formats — (1) a tree diagram (2) by means of phrase structure rules or rewrite rules, or (3) by means of labelled brackets:

(1) Jeeves will meet his employer at the castle (words are not immediate constituents, they are ultimate constituents).

(2a) Diagram

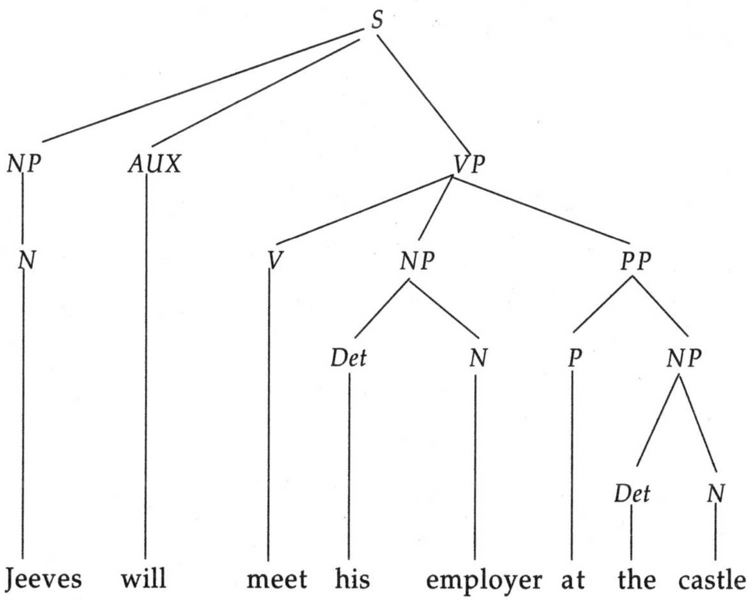

(2b)	(i)	*S*	*NP-AUX-VP*
	(ii)	*NP*	*(Det)-N*
	(iii)	*VP*	*V-NP-PP*
	(iv)	*PP*	*V-NP*
	(v)	*N*	Jeeves, employer castle
	(vi)	*V*	meet
	(vii)	*AUX*	will
	(viii)	*P*	at
	(ix)	*Det*	the, his

(2c) [*S* [*NP* [*N* Jeeves]] [*AUX* WILL] [*VP* [*V* meet]] [*NP* [*Det* his]] [*N* employer] [*PP* [*P* at]] [*NP* [*Det* the]] [*N* castle]]]]]

All the constituents, i.e. *VP*/*NP*/PP be proposed and it can be observed that not any string of words in the sentence can be preposed.

(3a) At the castle, Jeeves will meet his employer (*PP* is preposed)

(3b) His employer Jeeves will meet at the castle (*NP* is preposed)

(3c) Meet the employer at the castle, Jeeves will (indeed) (*VP* preposed)

In (3) above one can observe that constituents of a sentence like *NP* and *VP* can be preposed but not any string of words. And also, the fact that sentence in (3) and (1) have got the same underlying structure as shown in (2).

The module of the grammar regulating *NP* interpretation will be referred to as the Binding Theory.

An *NP* like John selects a referent from the universe of discourse, i.e. a lexical *NP* is able to select a referent by virtue of its inherent properties.

Pronouns do not have the inherent property to select a referent from the universe of discourse. For example, "him" need not refer to "John" — in a sentence without context — John killed him. It is actually "Pragmatics" which deals with such an aspect. Rather "him" and "John" cannot be co-referential is a matter of grammar. John killed himself — here in this sentence "himself" the reflexive, must refer to the subject, i.e. John.

In the above sentence John is called antecedent. And the reflexive, i.e. himself and the antecedent must agree with respect to their nominal features as the reflexive depends for its interpretation on the antecedent — there cannot be a sentence like "John killed herself" or "John killed themselves" as there is no AGREEMENT between the reflexive (anaphor) and the antecedent. Therefore, reflexives must be bound by an antecedent and the antecedent is the binder of the reflexive.

The referential expressions are inherently referential. John, the thief, etc. select a referent from the universe of discourse. Since R-expressions have independent reference, they do not need an antecedent and do not tolerate binding from another element. R-expressions must be free everywhere, e.g. John killed him. Here the pronoun "him" and R-expression John have got different referents — both are free (without binding).

Therefore, it can be concluded that anaphors need a local antecedent; pronouns may have an antecedent but must be free locally; and R-expressions must be free. These three principles of *NP* interpretation are referred to as Binding Theory.

In GB, grammar — internal modularity is carried as far as it can go; with some minor exceptions, all syntactic complexity results from the interaction of the following grammatical subsystems (Chomsky, 1981):

Bounding Theory — Which sets limits on the domain of movement rules.

Government Theory — Which defines the relation between the head of a construction and those categories dependent upon it.

Q Theory — Which deals with the assignment and functioning of thematic roles.

Binding Theory — Which links grammatical elements such as pronouns, anaphors, names and variables with their antecedents.

Case Theory — Which deals with the assignment of abstract case and its morphological realization.

Control Theory — Which determines the potential for reference of the abstract pronominal element PRO.

X-Bar Theory — Which constrains the base component of the grammar.

An example of binding theory offered in Newmeyer (1986) is shown on the facing fage.

Systemic Linguistics

According to this theory, language has to be considered as a system, which is to be analysed based on internal and external determinants of language system. The external determinant is the one that remains stable and the internal one, influenced by the external one, describes the evolution of language within. The concept proposed by Humboldt in nineteenth century and

Who does Mary think wants to shave himself

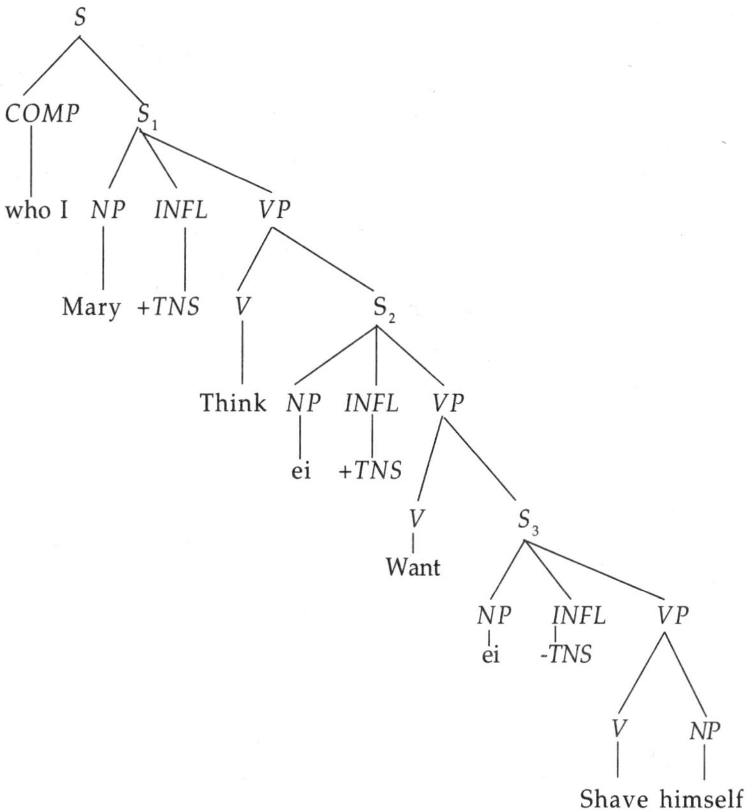

which goes against the principles of structuralism was further worked out by Melnikov.

Tagmemic Theory

Proposed and elaborated by Kenneth L. Pike (Pike 1967a) the theory was first published in 1954. It is a theory of "unit-in-context." Unlike other theories Tagmemic Theory (tagmeme is a "unit-in-context" with four cells) demands that context be considered at every step, that is, in all perception and experience and knowledge. Form must not be treated apart from meaning. Each unit of each level of each hierarchy — grammatical, phonological and referential — has a physical component. In tagmemic theory there is no semantic hierarchy abstracted away from all physical manifestation; the referential hierarchy is not a semantic one *per se*, but is a different and simultaneous structuring of the same stuff, which is also structured by the grammatical and phonological hierarchies. In this chapter I am rejecting all views of language or life which claim that *abstract* forms comprise basic reality (*Linguistic Concepts: An Introduction to Tagmemics*, 1982, Ch. 12).

4

Oriental vs. Occidental

Phonetics

PHONETICS was a fully developed and vast subject, so far as the Indian grammatical tradition is concerned (see Allen's book on Phonetics). There are five Prātiśākhyas[1] and thirty-one Śikṣās[2] that are available. Patañjali[3] records his observations regarding the major shift in academic atmosphere which was most probably due to the less longevity enjoyed by the people — during earlier time (*kalpa*) the brāhmaṇas were studying Vyākaraṇa and for them who had had good knowledge of phonetics, Veda was being pronounced (taking his observation[4] elsewhere it can be presumed that the order was — Śikṣā-Vyākaraṇa-Veda long before Patañjali), whereas now (i.e. around Patañjali's time) pupils, after learning Veda are hurried in enjoying family life and posing the question — we

1. *ṛgvedaḥ-ṛkprātiśākhyā; sāmavedaḥ-ṛktantravyākaraṇam; kṛṣṇayajurvedaḥ-taittirīyaprātiśākhyā; śuklayajurvedaḥ-vājasaneyaprātiśākhyā/ kātyāyanīyaprātiśākhyā; atharvavedaḥ-atharvaprātiśākhyā* ।

2. *śikṣāsaṁgrahaḥ* ।

3. *purā kalpe etadāsīt-saṁskārottarakālam brāhmaṇā vyākaraṇam smādhīyate, tebhyaḥ tattatsthānakaraṇanādānupradānajñebhyaḥ vaidikāḥ śabdā upadiśyante* । *adyatve na tathā* । *vedamadhītya tvaritā vaktāro bhavanti-vedānno vaidikāḥ śabdāḥ, lokānno laukikāḥ, anarthakam vyākaraṇam iti* । — *Mahābhāṣyam, paspaśāhnikam*

4. *vyākaraṇam nāmeyamuttarā vidyā* । *so 'sau chandaśśāstreṣvabhivinīta upalabhyādhigantumutsahate* । — *Mahābhāṣyam*, 1-2-32

learnt Vaidika *śabda*s from Veda, laukika *śabda*s from routine interaction with people, then Vyākaraṇa is useless.

Prātiśākhyas exclusively deal with Vedic phonetics whereas Śikṣā[5] deals with the norms of phonetics in general (i.e. both Vedic and secular). Among all the Śikṣās, *Pāṇinīya-Śikṣā* is considered to be the most authentic and popular. It is the disciples of Pāṇini who had compiled the available text as per the instructions they received from Pāṇini.

The generation of *varṇa*s (phonemes) is beautifully explained in *Pāṇinīya-Śikṣā*[6] — the *ātmā* (*antaḥkaraṇam*/the soul) gets the things associated with *buddhi* and employs the *manas* (mind) with a desire to express. Then the *manas* activates the *jaṭharāgni* (the fire that is there in the stomach or the fire of hunger), and in turn the *jaṭhara* stimulates the air upwards. Such an air touches the speech organs and different *varṇa*s are thus produced.

Unlike in the case of other languages across the globe, the authors of Śikṣā had insisted upon the perfect pronunciation of *varṇa*s. *Pāṇinīya-Śikṣā*[7] explains the concept clearly and naturally — a tigress shifts her cubs with the help of large teeth, without causing pain, fearing fall or cut — like that one

---

5. *atha śikṣām pravakṣyāmi pāṇinīyam matam yathā* ।
śāstrānupūrvam tadvidyādyathoktam lokavedayoḥ ॥
— *Pāṇinīya-Śikṣā, ślokaḥ* 1

6. *ātmā buddhyā sametyārthān mano yuṅte vivakṣayā* ।
manaḥ kāyāgnimāhanti sa prerayati mārutam ॥

sodīrṇo mūrdhnyabhihato vaktramāpadya mārutaḥ ।
varṇān janayate . . . . ॥ — *Pāṇinīya-Śikṣā*, 6 & 9
— *Vyākhyānam*, by Nageśabhaṭṭaḥ, *Laghuśabdenduśekharaḥ, Saṁjñāprakaraṇam*

7. *vyāghrī yathā haretputrān damṣṭrābhyām na ca pīḍayet* ।
bhītā patanabhedābhyām tadvadvarṇān prayojayet ॥
— *Pāṇinīya-Śikṣā, ślokaḥ* 25

should pronounce *varṇas*. And the flavour of philosophy is added even to the act of articulation[8] — the *varṇas* should be articulated in a no-non-clear and not-pressed manner. One would enjoy in *brahmaloka* through good articulation of *varṇas*.

As per the pronunciation of *hrasva, dīrgha* and *pluta*, Pāṇini had resorted to the natural cock's crow to explain the temporal aspect[9] — *u, u2, u3* — thus the *hrasva, dīrgha* and *pluta* of an *ac* has to be pronounced. Pāṇini preferred *u*, leaving behind *a* and *i*, in order to imitate the cock's crow.

In *Śikṣā* and *Mahābhāṣya*, a number of common speech defects, including the nasal pronunciation and lose utterance are enumerated. In the musical science[10] (Saṅgītaśāstra) different animals and birds are taken for explaining the art of articulation. *Śikṣā* has got the origin.

Eight places are there in the body where *varṇas* are produced according to *Śikṣā*[11] — chest, throat, roof of the mouth, root of the tongue, the teeth, nose, lips and palate.

---

8. *evam varṇāḥ prayoktavyā nāvyaktā na ca pīḍitāḥ* ।
samyagvarṇaprayogeṇa brahmaloke mahīyate ॥
— *Pāṇinīya-Śikṣā*, 31

9. *ūkālo 'jjhrasvadīrghaplutaḥ* । — *Pāṇini*, 1-2-27

10. *dhaivatam heṣate vājī niṣādam bṛmhate gajaḥ* ।
ajāvikam tu gāndhāram krauñcaḥ kvaṇati madhyamam ॥
ṣaḍjam mayūro vadati gāvastvṛṣabhabhāṣiṇaḥ ।
puṣpasādhāraṇe kāle pikaḥ kūjati pañcamam ॥
— *Amarakośaḥ*, 1-*śabdādivargaḥ*

udātte niṣādagāndhārāvanudātta ṛṣabhadhaivatau ।
svaritaprabhavā hyete ṣadjamadhyamapañcamāḥ ॥
— *Pāṇinīya-Śikṣā*, 12

11. *aṣṭau sthānāni varṇānāmuraḥ kaṇṭhaḥ śirastathā* ।
jihvāmūlam ca dantāśca nāsikoṣṭhau ca tālu ca ॥
— *Pāṇinīya-Śikṣā, ślokaḥ*, 13

Many more details are not being mentioned due to space considerations.

In Western linguistics, articulatory phonetics or phonetics is the study or description of *varṇa*s/speech sounds. The oral cavity (mouth), the nasal cavity, the pharynx (throat) and the region consisting of all these organs is called speech tract.[12] The velum (front and back), the dome, the alveolar ridge, the backs of the upper teeth, the cutting edges of the upper teeth and the upper lip — seven in total (eight in Pāṇiniyan system) are considered as the points of articulation.

The conspicuous difference between ancient Indian phonetics (*Śikṣā*) and modern phonetics is the insistence on perfect and similar pronunciation of each phoneme every time (except in the case of children and people who are weak due to old age or disease) by the former and non-insistence on such a norm by the latter — this does not mean that we must necessarily pronounce *P* in exactly the same way every time, and we do not.[13]

The importance of perfect pronunciation is discussed widely in *Śikṣā* and *Mahābhāṣya* (first two chapters). The common defects of speech (and imitation) are also enumerated and illustrated in the above books. In fact, it was the right and wrong pronunciation that prompted the Indian systemists to divide people into Āryas and *mlecchas*.[14] The term *mleccha* literally means a person who speaks unclearly/*apaśabda*s (i.e. other than Sanskrit).

12. Hocket Charles F., *A Course in Modern Linguistics*, pp. 63 & 69.

13. Ibid., p. 25.

14. *Paspaśāhnikam, Mahābhāṣyam*
āryamlecchādhikaraṇam, śābarabhāṣyam
mleccha=aspaṣṭabhāṣaṇe (bhvādi/curādi)
atha mliṣṭamavispaṣṭam, Amarakośaḥ, Pāṇini, 7-2-18

Padam and Word

Padam, which is the immediate constituent (*suptiṅantam padam* — Pāṇini 1-4-14) is a well defined unit of language. It is a group of *varṇa*s with specific sequence. *Vyākaraṇam*, since it deals exclusively and chiefly with word formation, is called *Padaśāstram*. As cataloguing of all the sentences is an impossible task so also that of words. Patañjali (in Paspaśā of *Mahābhāṣya*) employed an *arthavāda* (an unreal event useful in urging a person to do or not to do something) to stress the point. Bṛhaspati (the *guru* of *devatā*s) was the teacher and Indra (the king of *devatā*s) was the disciple. The time for pronouncing all the words was a thousand divine years. There was no end. Therefore, cataloguing all perfect *śabda*s (*pada*s) is not feasible. It was after pondering over all the options that Vaiyākaraṇas preferred to split the words — rather to offer sets of *prakṛti*s (roots) and *pratyaya*s (suffixes). Through combining the *prakṛti*s with *pratyaya*s in the prescribed manner one would get the perfect words fit for usage. Neither *prakṛti*s nor *pratyaya*s can be used independently — rules Patañjali in *Mahābhāṣya*.[15] Earlier to Pāṇini, there was fourfold categorization of *pada*s.[16] Pāṇini put them under two heads — *subantam* and *tiṅantam*, i.e. noun and verb. As has already been stated at the outset of this book, *Vyākaraṇam* is called *Padaśāstra*.

Pāṇini's way of offering the structure of words is twofold — in the former method both *prakṛti* and *pratyaya* are given by *ācārya* (Pāṇini) and the job left to the disciple is simply to combine both of them. This way is the most economical — Vaiyākaraṇas consider economizing a single *mātrā*[17] (roughly phoneme) on a

15. *na kevalā prakṛtiḥ prayoktavyā nāpi pratyayaḥ* ।
— *Mahābhāṣyam*, 1-2-64

16. *nāmākhyātopasarganipātāḥ* । — *Vājasaneyaprātiśākhyā*

17. *ekamātrālāghavam putrotsavam manyante vaiyākaraṇāḥ* ।
— *Paribhāṣā*

par with the birth of a (masculine) child. *Kṛ* (*du kṛñ — karaṇe*) is the root. It turns into *kartā, kartrī* and *kartṛ* with *tṛc- pratyaya, kṛtiḥ* with *ktin, kārakaḥ* with *ṇvul, karaḥ* with *ac, kāraḥ* with *aṇ, kārī* with *ṇini, kārayitā* with *ṇic, karoti* with *tiṅ, cikīrṣā* with *san*, etc. By prefixing *pra*, etc. *upasargas*[18] one would get *prahāra, āhāra, saṁhāra, vihāra, upahāra, apahāra, prabhavati, sambhavati*, etc. words.

On the other hand, readymade words (called *nipātas*) fit for usage are pronounced by *ācārya* and the job left for the disciple is to imagine the *prakṛti* and *pratyaya* thereof. *Śrotriyaṁśchando 'dhīte*[19] is a *sūtra* which prescribes a word *śrotriyaḥ* in the sense of "one who recites Veda." *Chandas* has got *śrotra-ādeśa* and *ghan* is the *pratyaya*. Similarly *kṣetriyac parakṣetre cikitsyaḥ*[20] is another *sūtra* which prescribes the word *kṣetrīyaḥ* (often seen in *Atharvaveda*) which means a disease that is to be treated in another body (another birth, i.e. incurable). Here *parakṣetra* is the *prakṛti* and *ghac* is the *pratyaya, para* has got *lopa*. In the above cases *n* and *c* are meant for specific *svara*.

No perfect definition could be offered for "word" by any modern linguist nor is it considered as a useful concept in linguistic analysis. A term, "morpheme" was borrowed from plant sciences to denote a part of a word (*prakṛti/pratyaya*) and the branch of linguistics which speaks about the formation of words is called morphology. Morphophonemics is *sandhi* and allomorphs are the resulting *sandhi* — alternants. Phoneme is the minimum linguistic unit without meaning whereas

---

18. *upasargeṇa dhātvartho balādanyatra nīyate* ।
prahārāhārasaṁhāravihāraparihāravat ॥
— *Siddhāntakaumudī, bhvādi*, 8-4-18

19. *śrotriyaṁśchando 'dhīte* । — *Pāṇini*, 5-2-84

20. *kṣetriyac parakṣetre cikitsyaḥ* । — *Pāṇini*, 5-2-92

morpheme is the minimum linguistic unit with meaning and neither is fit for usage — in the word "orderly" — order + ly — they are two morphemes. A word is a linguistic unit that has got some meaning and is fit to be used independently — order, chair, etc. In order to avoid problem with examples like *a, an,* the, some linguists redefined a word as a unit that has got space before and after (in print or script). Unlike in ancient linguistic science, words are not the immediate constituents of a sentence. Rather they are the ultimate constituents. The words of a sentence are organized heirarchically into bigger units called phrases. Jesperson explains that syntax proceeds from the inner aspect to the outer, while morphology proceeds from the outer to the inner. According to another scholar — "language has two sides — a formal side . . . concerned with the outer form of words and sentence, and a logical side . . . concerned with their inner meaning." Grammar deals with neither separately, but with the connections between them, these being the real phenomena of language.

Vākyam and Sentence

According to Indian grammarians *vākyam* is also a *śabda-saṁjñā*, name of a *śabda* like *pada* and *varṇa.* At operational level it is considered to be a group of words that satisfies the triplet of prerequisites, viz. *ākāṅkṣā* (mutual expectancy), *yogyatā* (compatibility) and *āsatti* (proximity). *Ākāṅkṣā* (a counter example for this faculty is "Rāvaṇa and Sītā," i.e. there is no mutual *ākaṅkṣā* between them) is needed to keep different words binding through the expectancy between them and this helps in expressing a unitary and complete meaning. *Yogyatā* is semantic competence — "Caitra is watering with fire" is a sentence without *yogyatā.* The words are necessarily to be pronounced in quick succession, as the ones pronounced with long interval in between fail to render (invoke) the *vākyārtha.* Therefore, *āsatti* or *sannidhi* is essential.

The words express their meaning (separately) and when they come in contact with each other, something more is seen emerging. The "more" (*viśeṣa* is called *vākyārtha* — the words that were known as *kartā, karma, kriyā,* etc. got, due to interaction, a binding relation called *viśeṣaṇa-viśeṣya-bhāva* (the relation of qualifier and qualified) or *saṁsarga* (of *padārthas*). The aspect of *vākya* and *vākyārtha* is exclusively discussed in *Mahābhāṣya*[21] and Vākyakāṇḍa of *Vākyapadīya.*[22]

As far as the modern linguistics is concerned the order is sentence — phrases and words rather than sentence-words, i.e. words are not the immediate constituents (IC) of a sentence as it is the case in ancient Indian theory. The analysis of phrases is taken care of by theories of phrase-structure such as X-bar theory.

Harris, while attempting to define "meaning" proposed that it should be done in such a way that the meaning of an utterance as a whole would be the sum of the meanings of the constituent morphemes. This proposition is ambiguous. Sentence-meaning can be the sum of word-meanings and not that of morpheme-meanings.

The morphological indications of syntactical linkage in English (when compared with other languages) are very few. In other languages such linkage is extensively indicated (Robert A. Hall Jr. 1969). Concord (congruence), government and cross-reference are the three main sub-types of agreement.

---

21. *padānām sāmānye vartamānānām yadviśeṣe 'vasthānam sa vākyārthaḥ* ।
— *Mahābhāṣyam*, 1-2-45

22. *sambandhe sati yattvanyadādhikyamupajāyate* ।
vākyārthameva tam prāhuranekapadasaṁśrayam ॥
— *Vākyapadīyam*, 2-42

Vāk and language

Right from Vedic literature *vāk* has been perceived and worshipped as a goddess[23] in India due to her philosophical outlook. Having mastered the Vyākaraṇa, one would get the *Brahman* (*jñāna*) — says Hari.[24]

On the other hand, Western scholars expressed different opinions about the form of language — an organism, social product, a product deposited in the mind of man, a workable system of signals and an activity of four kinds, i.e. speaking, listening, writing and reading.

Artha and Meaning

Vāk (*śabda*) and *artha* are inseparable according to Indian scholars. There cannot be any linguistic enquiry without reference to meaning.

On the Western front the early logicians-cum-linguists of Vienna circle (prominent among them was Wittgenstein, 1889–1951) hold that in logical syntax the meaning of a sign ought never to play a role. Earlier Alfred Taraka of Warsaw School of logicians, had employed some techniques and was successful in the formalization but without keeping away the meaning. He, in fact, felt that syntax must be supplemented by semantic concept. Bloomfield and his followers hold the opposite view.

Harris (1954, papers 8-9) opined that there is no independently known structure of meanings which exactly parallels linguistic structure. It is really amazing even to think

---

23. *devīm vācamajanayanta devāstām viśvarūpāḥ paśavo vadanti* ।
— *Ṛgvedaḥ*, 8-100-11

24. *tadvyākaraṇamāgamya parambrahmādhigamyate* ।
— *Vākyapadīyam*, 1-22

about the claim of certain modern linguists that they are primarily concerned with the three structural levels, viz. phonology, morphology and syntax, with complete disregard to meaning, the major function of language, and as such be considered as an integral part of linguistics.

At a later stage the harm done to linguistics by ignoring meaning and the importance of semantics (the analysis of meaning) was felt by Western scholars and they developed the same along with syntax. As the linguistic research advanced towards discourse/text analysis the semantic phenomenon like cohesion/coherence occupied the first place. (As is observed by some Western linguists the so-called theories in occidental theatre change very fast and it is very difficult to reckon upon a single theory as a sustainable and permanent one.)

The study (or analysis) of meaning is labelled "semantics" in modern linguistics. Semantics is not as systematic as it is in ancient linguistic study across the Indian subcontinent.

For Indian theorists *śabda* and *artha* are inseparable.[25] *Śabda, artha* and *jñāna* are non-different from each other. *Gauḥ* is the *śabda,* the same is *artha* and the same is *jñāna.*[26] Rather, for all practical purposes *śabda* renders the primary meaning through *abhidhā-vṛtti.* In case it is not acceptable, *lakṣaṇā-vṛtti* enters the scene (London is on river Thames — is not acceptable as the existence of a city on a stream of waters called Thames is simply not possible. So *abhidhā* is followed by *lakṣaṇā* to render the meaning that is acceptable — London is on the banks of river Thames) — *gaṅgāyāṁ ghoṣaḥ* (the village of herdsmen is in Ganges) is the popular example for *lakṣaṇā. Lakṣaṇā-vṛtti*

25. *vāgarthāviva sampṛktau* । — *Raghuvaṁśaḥ,* 1-1

26. *śabdārthapratyayānāmitaretarādhyāsātśaṅkarastatpravibhāgas-amyamātsarvabhūtarutajñānam* । — *Yogasūtram,* 3-17

enters the scene and renders *lakṣyārtha* (secondary meaning) the village of herdsmen (*ghoṣa* means a cowshed as well) is on the bank of Ganges. The purpose of such a usage (where the *vācyārtha* or primary meaning is not acceptable) is explained by *vyañjanā-vṛtti* and the *artha* thus achieved is called *vyaṅgyārtha* or *dhvani* (suggested meaning or implication) — the village of herdsmen is holy and cool. Here is a table to explain the order:

Śabda	**Artha**	**Vṛtti**	**Example**
Vācaka	*Vācya*	*Abhidhā*	*Gaṅgāyām ghoṣaḥ* (The village of herdsmen is in Ganges)
Lakṣaka	*Lakṣya*	*Lakṣaṇā*	*Gaṅgātīre ghoṣaḥ* (The village of herdsmen is on the bank of Ganges)
Vyañjaka	*Vyaṅgya/ Dhvani*	*Vyañjanā*	The village of herdsmen on the bank of Ganges is holy and cool.

Tātparya,[27] according to some is a separate *vṛtti*, whereas others include it in *vyañjanā*, e.g. *kākebhyo sarpiḥ rakṣyatām*[28] (let the ghee be protected from crows). Here in this case even a child understands that the word "crows" means crows, etc., i.e. dogs, cats and so on. Rather he takes it that the ghee has to be protected from any agent that is going to spoil the same.

Leonard Bloomfield observed this phenomenon — sometimes the practical feature that forces us to take a form in a transferred meaning, has been given by speech : Old Mr Smith is a fox — is bound to be taken in transferred meaning,

27. *tātparyārtho 'pi keṣucit* । — *Kāvyaprakāśaḥ*, 2-6

28. *kākebhyo rakṣyatām sarpiḥ iti bālo 'pi coditaḥ* ।
upaghātapare vākye na śvādibhyo na rakṣati ॥
— *Vākyapadīyam*, 2-312

because we do not call real foxes Mr or give them family-names.

Vyākaraṇam and Grammar

Vyākaraṇam includes grammar and not vice versa. Literally Vyākaraṇa means separation of (*sādhu*) *śabda*s from *apaśabda*s. In other words the system speaks of use and abuse of language. *Gauḥ* is a *śabda*, whereas *gāvī, goṇī, gotā, gopotalikā* (registered by Patañjali), etc. are *apaśabda*s. While transformation of meaning from the speaker to the listener is the same from *śabda*s as well as *apaśabda*s, Vyākaraṇaśāstra prescribes that use of *śabda*s fetches *dharma*.[29] Prātiśākhyas are those which exclusively deal with *vaidika-śabda*s and Vyākaraṇams are those which deal with *laukika-śabda*s only — this was the situation earlier to Pāṇini. Rather, *Pāṇinīya* which only is fit to be called a Vedāṅga (-Vyākaraṇam)[30] deals with *śabda*s of both *vaidika* and *laukika* in nature. *Vyākaraṇam* depends upon Veda and (*śiṣṭa*) *prayoga* — the usage (*prayogaśaraṇam vyākaraṇam*).

Pāṇini[31] was a *smartā* (registrar) of *śabda*s and not a *sraṣṭā* (creator) of *śabda*s. His work is the famous *Aṣṭādhyāyī*.

---

29. *samānāyāmarthāvagatau śabdaiścāpaśabdaiśca śāstreṇa dharmaniyamaḥ kriyate* ı — *Mahābhāṣyam, Paspaśāhnikam*

śiṣṭebhya āgamātsiddhā sādhavo dharmasādhanam ı
arthapratyāyanābhede viparītāstvasādhavaḥ ıı
— *Vākyapadīyam*, 1-27

30. *atha śabdānuśāsanam, keṣām śabdānām? laukikānām vaidikānām ca* ı — *Mahābhāṣyam, Paspaśāhnikam*

31. *tasmānnibadhyate śiṣṭaiḥ sādhutvaviṣayā smṛtiḥ* ı — *Vākyapadīyam*, 1-29

avicchedena śiṣṭānāmidam smṛtinibandhanam ı — *Vākyapadīyam*, 1-142

Eight aspects are discussed in *Aṣṭādhyāyi* —

Śabda	-	1. *Prakṛti* and *pratyaya* 2. *Pada* and *vākya*
Artha	-	1. *Prakṛtipratyayārtha* 2. *Padavākyārtha*
Sambandha between *Śabda* and *artha*		1. *Kārya-kāraṇa-bhāva* 2. *Yogyatā*
Prayojanam (Purpose)		1. *Arthajñāna* 2. *Dharma*

Since cataloguing all the *vākyas* (in Sanskrit) is an impossible task, *padas* are taken for analysis. There too it is difficult to list out the *padas* and hence the *prakṛtipratyayavibhāga*.[32]

Pāṇini's *Aṣṭādhyāyī* is both descriptive and prescriptive in nature in that it offers various *pratyayas* to be added to various *prakṛtis* and in some cases offers readymade *śabdas* from which the *prakṛti* and *pratyaya* are to be deduced.

Pāṇini initially offers the alphabet in fourteen *sūtras* and it is traditionally believed that he received the same from Lord Maheśvara. He dealt exclusively with phonetics in *Pāṇinīya-Śikṣā*.

The analysis of *padas* (divided into *prakṛti* and *pratyaya* — may be called morphemes), *vākya* (syntax/*kāraka* theory) and *mahāvākya* (discourse) is conspicuous in *Aṣṭādhyāyī*. Prescription of the form of *śabdas* (*śabda* everywhere means *sādhu-śabda*)

32. *apoddhārapadārthā ye ye cārthāḥ sthitalakṣaṇāḥ* ।
anvākhyeyāśca ye śabdā ye cāpi pratipādakāḥ ॥
kāryakāraṇabhāvena yogyabhāvena ca sthitāḥ ।
dharme ca pratyaye cāṅgam sambandhāssādhvasādhuṣu ॥
te liṅgaiśca svaśabdaiśca śāstre 'sminnupavarṇitāḥ ।
— *Vākyapadīyam*, 1-24, 25 & 26

and not meanings is the task that was fulfilled by Pāṇini with perfection and brevity that are unsurpassable. At times, he may say — "in the sense" (*cārthe dvandvaḥ, anekamanyapadārthe, tasyāpatyam,* etc.) and it means that the *śabda* is seen being used in such and such an *artha* (*artha* is taken care of by *Nirukta*). Therefore, Vyākaraṇa is also called *Śabdānuśāsanam* or *Śabdaśāstram*. On the whole, *Pāṇinīya* can be called a prescriptive grammar (translation) in that it prescribes *śabdas* in spite of the description of most of the *śabdas*. It may also be noted that the analysis of *padas*, i.e. offering *prakṛti* and *pratyaya*, is not real and as such it may vary from Pāṇini to Śākaṭāyana to Śākalya. But the form of the *padam* won't change. This is so because it is *pada-sphoṭa* at some level and *vākya-* (*-jāti*) *sphoṭa* in the conclusion that is the real candidate that transforms meaning (*mahāvākya-sphoṭa* and *mahāvākya-dhvani* are also acceptable at higher levels).

Strictly speaking, as per the evidence available in *Aṣṭādhyāyī*, Pāṇini did not, anywhere, say that *svara* (accent) is applicable only to *vaidika-śabdas*[33] (he did not institute an *adhikārasūtra*, like *chandasi*, before *svara-prakriyā*, which would have made the *svara* applicable only to *vaidika-śabdas*). Rather *svara* in *laukika-bhāṣā* is not the deciding factor of meaning as it is in *vaidika-bhāṣā*. *Svara* in *laukika-bhāṣā* is called *ekaśruti*, which insinuates that no difference of *udātta*, etc. is felt.

Perfection and brevity are the hallmarks of Pāṇini. *Aṣṭādhyāyī* is supported by *Vārtikas* of Kātyāyana et al. and a vast scholium (commentary) called *Mahābhāṣya* by Patañjali. Pāṇini, Kātyāyana and Patañjali are called *munitrayam* (the trio of sages) and the subject is "Munitrayam Vyākaraṇam." If there

33. *indraśatrurityādau veda eva na kāvye svaro viśeṣapratītikṛt*
— *Kāvyaprakāśaḥ*, 2-19

seems to be any difference of opinion among the three, the latter's opinion prevails (*yathottaram munīnām prāmāṇyam*).

Harris (1954) holds that "a grammar may be viewed as a set of instructions, which generates the sentences of the language." His follower Chomsky felt that a generative grammar was required to relate signals to the semantic interpretation of these signals.

In the light of the above and other views of Western linguists we can safely conclude that Vyākaraṇam is built on usages already available and also useful in identifying the right *śabda*s whereas grammar of modern linguistics is meant for generating sentences.

Language Acquisition

Indian intelligentsia did not probe much into the aspect of language acquisition by a child. All they say is a child learns the use of language by observation of the speech and related act that takes place between two elders. When a sentence like *gām ānaya*[34] (fetch the cow) is used, the listener fetches the cow, whereas a sentence like *gām naya* (take the cow away) prompts the listener to do the opposite. The philosophical attitude of Indian sages might have been the cause that made them confined to use and abuse of language (by grown-ups) rather than the acquisition of language by a child.

On the other hand, the Western linguists had devoted much of the literature to "child language," as their goals of the investigation of language are quite different, i.e. mundane in nature.

---

34. *prayojyaprayojakavr̥ddhavyavahāram paśyatā bālena prayojyasya pravr̥tyā tasya jñānamanumāya copasthitatvācchabdameva kāraṇatvena gr̥hītvā . . . .* — *Laghumañjūṣā, pr̥.* 23

Pratibhā (Competence) and Vyavahāra (Performance)

While taking up a detailed discussion of the concept (or definition) of a *vākya* and *vākyārtha*, Bhartṛhari[35] speaks about the understanding of *śabda* (both *dhvani* and *varṇa*, i.e. meaningless and meaningful) by non-humans and humans. It is a thing called *abhyāsa* (or innate/inherent capacity of mind) which enables both children and non-humans (birds and animals) to understand *śabda*. Such an *abhyāsa*, clarifies Hari, is the one that is inherited from earlier birth and not attained through the study of Śāstras in this birth. *Abhyāsa* is the cause of *pratibhā*, which is helpful in the understanding — after such a *śabda* such an act has to be undertaken. That's why Mīmāṁsakas proved that *kārya* (act/activity) is *vākyārtha*. *Abhyāsa*, *saṁketa* and *samaya* are synonyms.[36]

Hari clearly states that *pratibhā* is the cause of *vyavahāra*[37] (day-to-day activity), and nobody, even the non-humans and children, can get on without *pratibhā* attained in this birth through *saṁketa* of elders or the one inherited from earlier birth.

Elaborating the concept of *pratibhā*, Hari[38] asks who caused the call of a male-cukoo into *pañcama-svara* during *madhumāsa*

---

35. *kākebhyo rakṣyatām sarpiḥ iti bālo 'pi coditaḥ* ।
upaghātapare vākye na śvādibhyo na rakṣati ॥
— *Vākyapadīyam*, 2-312

36. *abhyāsāt pratibhā hetuḥ śabdassarvo 'paraissmṛtaḥ* ।
bālānām ca tiraścām ca yathārthapratipādane ॥
— *Vākyapadīyam*, 2-117

37. *anāgamaśca so 'bhyāsaḥ samayaḥ kaiścidiṣyate* ।
anantaramidam kāryamasmādityupadarśanam ॥
— *Vākyapadīyam*, 2-118

38. *sākṣācchabdena janitām bhāvanānugamena vā* ।
itikartavyatāyām tām na kaścidativartate ॥

→

(spring)? Who trained the spider in making a cobweb? A cat eats a rat, a dog loves its master, tiger and cow express hatred at each other, rhino, and other animals swim in water — who prompted these non-humans to behave like that? — it is beginningless *pratibhā*. Therefore, *abhyāsa* is the cause of *pratibhā*, which is in turn identified with *śabda* (or *vākyārtha*).

Competence and performance (*langue* and *parole* — Saussure) in modern linguistics refer to language knowledge (the inner capacity) and language use respectively. There is slight difference between Chomsky and Saussure in the interpretation — the latter thinks that most syntactic relations were part of *parole* rather than *langue.*

It is difficult to say that competence and *pratibhā* are identical *in toto* — *pratibhā* is well defined and elaborated (see commentary on 152 Vākyakāṇḍa, *Vākyapadīya*) while the concept of competence is not so. Dell Hymes (1971: 16) coined "Communicative Competence" — a term for speaking and hearing capabilities of a person. Some generative grammarians tried to downplay the use of such a term.

Performance also is not an equivalent of *vyavahāra in toto.* In Indian grammatical tradition, *vyavahāra* or *prayoga* or *loka* means *śiṣṭa-vyavahāra* (refer *Mahābhāṣyam* on p. 6-1-109, *ārya*s are *śiṣṭa*s) and not the usage of language by anybody. Except differences only in the form of some *śabda*s (not meaning) and

---

→ *svaravṛttim vikurute madhau puṁskokilasya kaḥ?*
jantvādayaḥ kulāyādikaraṇe kena śikṣitāḥ?

āhāraprītyapadveṣaplavanādikriyāsu kaḥ?
jātyanvayaprasiddhāsu prayoktā mṛgapakṣiṇām?

svabhāvacaraṇābhyāsayogādṛṣṭopapāditām ।
viśiṣṭopahitām ceti pratibhām ṣaḍvidhām viduḥ ॥
— *Vākyapadīyam*, 2-146, 149, 150, 152

svara in Vedic literature, no change in the form of *śabda* is permitted in so far as Sanskrit language is concerned. Probably this might be the reason why Sanskrit became the only language that fits machines (computers).

On the other hand, there are several Englishes (British, American, Indian, etc.), and speakers of each variety claim that the one they speak is standard. The modern linguists admit that language changes (naturally) due to many factors — social, cultural, etc. This is true even in the case of Indian vernaculars, like Telugu, Hindi, etc. This tendency had compelled the language scholars to go for standardization of language. It may be noted that Sanskrit, in spite of the fact that it was a spoken language, retained the form (and meaning) intact. It is also a fact that Sanskrit adapted some words from other languages also (for example Persian words like *anaphā, sunaphā, duradhurā* in *Jyotiṣa-Śāstra*).

5

Discourse Analysis — East and West

A DISCOURSE or *mahāvākya* is the very unit of language. Any stretch of language, beyond a sentence is a discourse. A great deal of work, which is, perhaps, unnoticed by the linguists outside the Indian subcontinent, had been done hundreds of years ago, by Indian philosophers of various schools, viz. Mīmāṁsā, Vyākaraṇa, Nyāya, etc. pertaining to the analysis of a discourse. It would, no doubt, run into volumes, if an exhaustive account of the material related to the present subject is to be given.

In this chapter I shall make an attempt to put in a nutshell the chief concepts of ancient Indian and other linguists pertaining to discourse, so that the linguists in both Eastern and Western hemispheres would be benefited.

The Indian scholarship has not been lagging behind, so far as the discourse analysis is concerned.

Each of the *śāstra*s and *darśana*s is built depending upon the theory of discourse. The founders of various systems had exploited the unique feature of *ekavākyatā*/onesentenceness/ cohesion, which is the criterion of discourse and composed voluminous treatises of grammar, jurisprudence, etc.

Kumārila's verse reads in *Tantravārtikā*:

svārthabodhe samāptānām aṅgāṅgitvavyapekṣayā ।
vākyānāmekavākyatvam punassaṁhatya jāyate ॥

Vākyaikavākyatā or one-sentenceness among (sub) sentences, which are full with their own meaning, would be born due to mutual expectancy based on the relation of constitute and constituent. The cohesion in a discourse is called *vākyaikavākyatā*, which corresponds to *padaikavākyatā* in a sentence.

Jaimini (fifth century BCE), the founder of Vākyaśāstra or Mīmāṁsā, as it is widely known, had, perhaps, for the first time defined a discourse thus — *arthaikatvādekam vākyam sākāṅkṣām ced vibhāge syāt* (if a single purpose is served or a single unitary sense is conveyed by the entire unit, and if the sub-sentences, when separated, are found to be wanting, it is a discourse). In this maxim the term *vākya* denotes a *mahāvākya* also.

It may be noted that all the prerequisites, viz. mutual expectancy, compatibility and proximity, needed by words to form a sentence, are also invariably needed by the sub-sentences to form a Discourse. The word in a sentence corresponds to the sub-sentence/*avāntaravākyam* in a discourse/*mahāvākyam*.

Here is a Vedic discourse, where the aforesaid rule is applied — one desirous of heaven must sacrifice with *darśa* and *pūrṇamāsa*. one has to perform the sacrifice consisting of *iṭ*. One has to perform the sacrifice consisting of *samit*. One has to perform the sacrifice consisting of *tanūnapāt*.

In the above passage, the first sentence is called *aṅgi-vākya* and the rest *aṅga-vākya*s. The former expects the latter to explain the procedure of performing the *darśapūrṇamāsayāga*. The expectancy is called *kathambhāvākāṅkṣā*. On the other hand, the latter expects the former to tell the result of performing the *iṭ*, and other sacrifices. The expectancy is called *phalākāṅkṣā*. Such a mutual expectancy is called *aṅgāṅgi-bhāva* or the relation of constitute and constituent. It is this relation that connects both parts of the said discourse and thus keeps up cohesion called *vākyaikavākyatā*, which results in rendering a unitary meaning. The passage can be abridged thus — one desirous of heaven should sacrifice with *darśa* and *pūrṇamāsa*, consisting of *iṭ*, *samit* and *tanūnapāt*.

The Vedāntins have closely followed in the footsteps of Mīmāṁsakas, so far as the *mahāvākya* is concerned. Vedavyāsa, the author of *Brahmasūtras*, had put his speculation in a nutshell — *tattu samanvayāt* (1-1-4, the *Brahman* can be known by knitting together Upaniṣadic sentences). Since a single purpose is served by all the Upaniṣads, they can be treated as a single *mahāvākya*. There are different schools of Vedānta, propounded by Śaṅkara, Rāmānuja, Madhva, etc. But none of them disagrees with the said theory. Śaṅkara declares under the maxim *janmādyasya* : *vedāntavākyakusumagrathanārthatvā vedāntasūtrāṇām, vedāntavākyāni sūtrairudāhṛtya vicāryante* (the purpose of *Vedāntasūtras* (*sūtra* means thread as well) is to string together the flowers of Upaniṣadic sentences, the sentences are illustrated and discussed by the *sūtras*). As all the sentences keep harping on the same thing (i.e. *Brahman*) an Upaniṣad can be taken as a unit, i.e. Discourse/*mahāvākya*.

The commentators on *Brahmasūtras* had enumerated six purports — deciding factors (*tātparyanirṇāyakas*) in support of the said *sūtra*. These factors are useful in deciding whether a given text can be taken as a single unit or not . . . .

> *upakramopasaṁhārāvabhyāso 'pūrvatā phalam* ।
> *arthavādopapattī ca liṅgam tātparyanirṇaye* ॥

> introduction and conclusion, repetition, novelty, result, commendation/condemnation and argument are the factors useful in deciding the purport of a passage.

Pāṇini, the grammatical genius, in his maxim — *vibhāṣā sākāṅkṣe,* had observed the change of verbal form, when two or more sentences with mutual expectancy are used. *Smarasī kṛṣṇa, vane vatsyāmaḥ* (or *avasāma*) *tatra gāścariṣyāmaḥ* (*acārayāma*) (would you recollect Kṛṣṇa, we used to live in the forest and used to take cows for grazing there) — is a discourse given as an example of this *sūtra*. The preceding *sūtras, na yadi* and *abhijñavacane lṛṭ,* are also pronounced by Pāṇini in the same context. As it is apparent in the first *sūtra, ākāṅkṣā* or mutual expectancy among sub-sentences is the criterion for the construction of the chain of *sūtras*.

Keeping the same idea in mind, Bhartṛhari, the author of *Vākyapadīyam,* had given the following description of a *mahāvākya* —

> *vākyānām samudāyaśca ya ekārthaprasiddhaye*
> *sākāṅkṣāvayavaḥ . . .* (2-76)

> a group of sentences, which is meant to serve a single purpose and in which the parts are found to be possessing mutual expectancy . . . is a *mahāvākya.*

It is also obvious that the verse gets its orientation from the definition provided by Jaimini.

Implicit is the theory of discourse, in the works related to Nyāya and Vaiśeṣika, when the five-membered-syllogism or *nyāyamahāvākya* is analysed. The syllogism is employed in order to enable others to have the inferential cognition. Inference/ *anumāna* occupies a very important place in both Nyāya and Vaiśeṣika systems of philosophy, when compared with other means of knowledge (*pramāṇas*). The said syllogism is technically called *parārthānumāna*/Nyāya. A person, having himself ascertained by frequent observation, the generalization — wherever there is smoke, there is fire, as in a kitchen —

approaches a mountain and finding smoke there remembers the aforesaid generalization and confirms the existence of fire on the mountain. The knowledge produced in this process, i.e. the mountain has smoke accompanied by fire, is called consideration/*parāmarśa*. This is one's own inference or *svārthānumāna*. When one, after inferring fire from smoke, employs a five-membered syllogism in order to enlighten another person, it is called *parārthānumāna* (inference for others). The five members are as follows — 1. Proposition, 2. Reason, 3. Example, 4. Application, and 5. Conclusion. The following are the five sentences representing the said members — The mountain is fiery; as it has smoke; wherever smoke there is fire, as in a kitchen; this is so; hence this is fiery. Here the group of five sentences is a logical discourse/*nyāya-mahāvākya*. As it is obvious, no sub-sentence from the above group can render a finite meaning and each sub-sentence has got expectancy. Thus connected both at syntactic and semantic levels, they form a discourse. With slight difference in the naming of the members, both Kaṇāda and Akṣapāda, the founder-sages of Vaiśeṣika and Nyāya systems of philosophy, had defined and expounded the Nyāya-theory. Kaṇāda named the limbs/*avayava*s as follows — *pratijñāpadeśanidarśanānusandhānapratyāmnāyāḥ*. Akṣapāda named thus — *pratijñāhetūdāharaṇopanayanigamanāni*.

In rhetorical works, the following terms are used in the sense of a discourse — *śabda, vākyam, mahāvākyam, prabandhaḥ,* and *vākovākyam*. Viśvanātha, in his famous work *Sāhityadarpaṇa* defines a discourse/*mahāvākya* thus — a group of sentences is a discourse (*vākyoccayo mahāvākyam*). He elaborates — having mutual expectancy, compatibility and proximity only. *Rāmāyaṇa, Mahābhārata* and *Raghuvaṁśa* are the examples offered by the author. The same idea was expressed by the famous Mīmāṁsaka of eighth century, Kumārilabhaṭṭa in his work *Tantravārtika* thus — so long as the cohesion continues to penetrate and a single purpose is served, the sentences come under a single *mahāvākya*/discourse . . . thus the *mahāvākya*s like *Mahābhārata* are to be commented.

It is obvious that Jagannāthapaṇḍitarāja of seventeenth century had closely followed the theory of discourse, embedded in various systems of Indian philosophy, while defining a *kāvya*, i.e. a *śabda* with aesthetic sense is a *kāvya* (*ramaṇīyārthapratipādakaśabdaḥ kāvyam*). It's no doubt a fact that the term *śabda* is employed to denote a phoneme/morpheme/word/sentence/discourse, etc. Here, since a single sentence, much less the rest of the factors preceding the same, cannot be legitimately called a *kāvya*, which is generally accepted and referred to a group of sentences, a discourse and a discourse only, it can be argued, is referred to by the term *śabda*. Jagannātha refers to *mahāvākya-dhvani* (the suggestive meaning of a discourse) — *mahāvākyadhvanera vāntaradhvanibhiḥ,* etc.

Bhojadeva in his famous work, *Śṛṅgāraprakāśa*, declares — a *mahāvākya*/discourse which eventually urges a person to perform/refrain from, an act is called a *prabandha* (*vidhiniṣedhāvagatiheturmahāvākyam prabandhaḥ*). This is said so with the generally accepted theory in mind that any stretch of language eventually rests either in urging a person in doing (*vidhi*/injunction) or refraining from (*niṣedha*/censure) an act. The commending/condemning sentences are also connected with injunction/censure either directly or indirectly.

Now I shall venture upon the task of summarizing the concepts of Western scholars regarding discourse. According to Aristotle — rhetoric is the theory and practice of persuasion by means of reasoned discourse. Earlier to him Plato also considered rhetoric as the art of rational discourse. Rhetorical theory, therefore, lays stress on logically sequenced verbal communication. Aristotle's consideration of an ordered chunk of rhetoric is thus — introduction, statement, argument and epilogue.

Zellig Harris was the first in modern era to recognize the necessity of linguistic investigation beyond a sentence. In 1955 he proposed a form of transformational analysis of a discourse. He put forward structural equivalence and distribution of sentence in combination. He was the first to go beyond structuralism. Harris argues that key words of the text, occurring many times, form such a class and therefore the neighbouring ones that also occur in identical environments form another class. So a text can be analysed in terms of equivalence classes. He illustrates the concept. It seems from the later linguistic works that the analysis put forth by Harris is not exemplary.

Linder Kay Jones summarizes some of the theories related to discourse analysis — cohesion describes the semantic unity of a text. Some of the typical cohesive relations studied by Halliday and Hasan are anaphora across sentences, lexical repetition, the use of definite articles, ellipses, conjunctions, etc. For them cohesion explains the semantic unity of text, totally apart from grammatical constituent structure. Indeed, Halliday and Hasan deny that there is any constituent structure for units as paragraph. They claim that the sentence is the largest unit that has constituent structure. They believe that these paragraphs and discourses are fundamentally different kinds of linguistic things from words, clauses and sentences. Tagmetics makes the opposite claim, that they are the same type of linguistic things; words, clauses, sentences, paragraphs and discourses are simply at different hierarchical levels of organization. Tagmetics states that there is constituent structure at each of these levels. In tagmetic theory, a section is a level of structure between paragraph and entire discourse (or text). It usually comprises more than one paragraph although there is nothing theoretically amiss about describing a one paragraph text as, simultaneously, a paragraph, a section and a text. In tagmetic theory higher levels than sentence include paragraph, section and text.

Richard Hurting had begun his discussion with the question — what is a discourse theory about? Is discourse, i.e. a string of successive sentences (where sentence is taken to be the structural equivalent of "utterance") a natural unit of language? Then he goes to explain his idea thus — "in natural speech communication discourse appears to involve units larger than the single sentence or utterance. Thus it is the set of successive utterances that we shall call discourse and the subject matter of a theory of discourse. Though discourses are variable in length and complexity, they do appear to be bounden, that is, finite in length; just as in the case of sentences that fact appears to be a phenomenon, which is due to perceptual and social context limitations rather than anything in the formal structure of discourse, discourse can be monologues, dialogues or multipersonal interchanges. Perhaps, most importantly, a discourse appears to have topical or logical structure. Successive utterances in a discourse appear to be linked on the basis of such a topical or logical structure. It is precisely these links, which a theory of discourse must account for." And it can be deduced from the above argument that a string of successive utterances, which are topically or logically connected, is called a discourse. Elsewhere, in the same article, the author states that a discourse is not definable — our discussion of discourse so far has assured that the unit of analysis was clearly isolable and that its boundaries were clearly defined. Unlike the sentence, whose boundaries appear intimately clear, the discourse unit is not as clearly definable. The linguistic grammar of discourse operates on the premise that given a discourse, it can provide the correct interpretation for that discourse.

On the contrary, the authors of *Introduction to Text Linguistics* opine that since discourse is definable as a situation or event sequence in which various participants present texts as discourse actions, we can consider communication through discourse as an instance of interactive-planning (C.F. Bruce & Newman 1978).

Interestingly, Michel Stubbs categorically emphasizes that no one is in a position to write a comprehensive account of discourse-analysis.

To sum up, the scholars of Indian philosophy hold identical opinion regarding a *mahāvākya*/discourse, whereas the linguists of the West have difference of opinion about the same. Moreover, the former have very clear understanding in all aspects of a discourse and the latter have got a somewhat vague idea of the very linguistic unit. The Western linguists, it seems, have not at all consulted the works of Oriental origin, so far as the present subject is concerned. There are, no doubt, similarities in the thinking of both the sides, as it is in the case of logical syllogism.

6

Inference, Syllogism and the Logical Discourse

Among the four means of knowledge accepted by the Nyāya system of Indian philosophy, inference occupies a very important position. Many a time the Logicians or Naiyāyikas are identified with inference or *anumāna* by other systemists. An inference is the application of general truth to a particular instance. *Anumā, anumānam, anumānaḥ, anumitiḥ, anumitam* are synonyms.

Inference is the peculiar cause of a judgement; judgement is the knowledge that springs from *parāmarśa* or consideration; and consideration is the knowledge of reason as distinguished by invariable concomitance, or *vyāpti*. For instance, the knowledge that this mountain has smoke which is invariably accompanied by fire is consideration, while the knowledge form of it, that the mountain is fiery is judgement or *anumiti*. Invariable concomitance is the certainty of association that wherever there is smoke, there is fire. The existence of an invariably concomitant thing on objects like mountain makes it the characteristic of a *pakṣa* or receptacle.

The chapters on inference contain the science of Indian logic as developed and skillfully dovetailed into the general system of metaphysics evolved by the Vaiśeṣikas. *Anumāna* or inference is the instrument; *anumiti* the resulting judgement; and *parāmarśa* the intermediate operation. *Anumiti* is thus said to depend upon *parāmarśa*. This *parāmarśa* occupies a very important place in Nyāya/logic; because once a valid *parāmarśa* is obtained, a sound conclusion or *anumiti* necessarily and immediately follows, just as cloth is produced as an invariable consequence of the motion of the loom. Hence Nyāya writers mainly devote themselves to a discussion of this *parāmarśa* and its two constituent parts *vyāpti* and *liṅga*. *Liṅga* or *hetu* is the thing from which the existence of another thing invariably concomitant with it, is inferred. *Vyāpti* is thus invariable concomitance existing between the *liṅga* and the other thing inferred from it, namely *sādhya* (see English Introduction to *Tarkasaṁgraha*).

It will be clear from the above that an inference when simplified always consists of three terms denoting respectively *sādhya, hetu* and their mutual relation of invariable concomitance, any two of which, when given, necessarily lead to a knowledge of the third, viz. *vyāpti*. Of these the *sādhya* is, of course, the thing which is always to be proved; and consequently the other two terms, *hetu* and the *sādhya-hetu-sambandha* or *vyāpti* must be known before any inference is possible. In the Aristotelian syllogism they correspond to the first two premises which, being connected together by a common middle term, lead to the conclusion; but the Aristotelian syllogism is defective in so far as it merely implies this connection between the two premises, and has no separate premise to express it. The Nyāya syllogism, on the other hand, actually expresses this connection between the two terms denoting *hetu* and *vyāpti* into one; that is, it does not merely state the two terms or premises separately, and then at once jumps to the conclusion, but after stating them fully gives a third premise which combines the previous two terms, and thus gives a unity as it were to the two separate cognitions of *hetu* and *vyāpti*. This combined premise is called *parāmarśa*, which immediately gives rise to the conclusion and is therefore said to be its *karaṇa*.

It must be noted that both the systems of Nyāya and Aristotle, though widely differing in their ultimate forms, are really founded on identical analysis of our thinking process. The two systems materially agree with each other until we arrive at the two cognitions expressed by Aristotle in the form of major and minor premises, and by the Naiyāyikas as *vyāpti* and *pakṣadharmatā* respectively. But from this point they diverge, chiefly on account of their different ways of combining these two cognitions and the divergence, though slight at first, ultimately leads to the forms of syllogism in the two systems. Aristotle first cognizes *hetu* as invariably concomitant with *sādhya* (in the major premise), and then finds this invariably concomitant *hetu* in a particular place in the minor; that is he first makes sure of *vyāpti* as a general truth, and then determines the existence of this *sādhya-vyāpya-hetu* on the *pakṣa*. The Naiyāyika reverses the order, by first determining the *hetu* on *pakṣa*, and then joining to it the notion of invariable concomitance, which, being derived from past experience, is remembered as soon as the *hetu* is perceived on the *pakṣa*. In Aristotle's system, *vyāpti* is determined first and then *pakṣadharmatā*; in Nyāya first *pakṣadharmatā* of the *hetu* is known and then the recollected notion of *vyāpti* is added to it. To adopt Sanskrit terminology, the combination of the two notions, i.e. the *parāmarśa* is expressed in Nyāya as *vyāptiviśiṣṭapakṣadharmatā*; while Aristotle would probably have described it as *pakṣadharmatāviśiṣṭavyāpti*, if, of course, he had laid down any third premise corresponding to *parāmarśa-vākya*. As a matter of fact we do not find this last form in Aristotle's syllogism, because the mixture of the two notions of *vyāpti* and *pakṣadharmatā*, designated *parāmarśa*, is only implied and not expressed. If, however, we introduce a premise into a latter syllogism corresponding to *parāmarśa*, we shall find that it assumes exactly the form indicated above, viz. *pakṣadharmatā-viśiṣṭa-vyāpti*. Take for example:

> All men are mortal;
> Socrates is a man;
> Socrates is mortal.

A Naiyāyika will put this as :

> Humanity (*manuṣyatvam*) is invariably concomitant with mortality (*martyatva-vyāptam*)
> There is humanity in Socrates;
> Therefore there is mortality in Socrates.

This syllogism is defective according to Nyāya, because just before the conclusion there is wanting of a step combining the two premises into one proposition. This *parāmarśa* would be — "the humanity in Socrates is invariably concomitant with mortality"; that is, we cognize *manuṣyatva* not as *martyatva-vyāpya* generally, but as *martyatva-vyāpya* in a particular individual, Socrates. In other words, the *vyāpti* which was first universal is here limited by *pakṣadharmatā*, i.e. *pakṣadharmatā-viśiṣṭa-vyāpti*. On the other hand, the same argument put in the Nyāya syllogism would be —

> *devadatto martyaḥ* (*martyatvaviśiṣṭaḥ*) *manuṣyatvāt* । *yo yo manuṣyaḥ sa sa martyatvaviśiṣṭaḥ* । *yathā yajñadattaḥ tathā cāyam devadattaḥ* । (*martyatvavyāpyamanuṣyatvaviśiṣṭaḥ*) *tasmāttathā* (*devadattaḥ martyaḥ*) ।

The only difference between this and the former syllogism is that here in the fourth step, i.e. *parāmarśa*, we predicate *martyatvavyāpyamanuṣyatvaviśiṣṭatva* of Devadatta, while in the former one we predicated *martyatvavyāpyatva* of *devadattaniṣṭha-manuṣyatva*. The result, of course, is the same, and the conclusion is as valid in the one as in the other syllogism.

7

Āryas and Purism of Language

THE term *ārya* is formed by adding the suffix *ṇyat* by *ṛhalorṇyat* (Pāṇini 3-1-124) on the *ṛ* (*gatau* = to go). Under *pṛṣodarādīni yathopadiṣṭam* (Pāṇini 6-3-109), Patañjali widely discusses the concept of Ārya [compare with Āryans defined in Mein Kampf of the German dictator; even *svastikā* mentioned in Paspaśā of *Mahābhāṣya* was also borrowed by the so-called Āryans; also see *Amarakośa* — *āryāvartaḥ puṇyabhūmiḥ madhyam vindhyahimāgayoḥ* — Āryāvarta or Puṇyabhūmi is the land between Vindhya and Himālaya; also *Manusmṛti* —

> *āsamudrācca pūrvasmāt āsamudrācca paścimāt* ।
> *tayorevāntarā giryoḥ āryāvartam pracakṣate* ॥

The land surrounded by sea on east and west and by mountains, viz. Himālaya and Vindhya, in north and south is called Āryāvarta] and Āryāvarta in connection with the language that has to be taken authoritatively. The brāhmaṇas[1] living across the length and breadth of Āryāvarta were leading a very systematic and ascetic life and were concerned about the purity of speech since it fetches *dharma*, which in turn would lead to the attainment of *mokṣa* (literally relief from worldly bindings) — union with *Brahman*. The brāhmaṇas of Āryāvarta

---

1. *etasminnāryāvarte nivāse ye brāhmaṇāḥ kumbhīdhānyā alolupā agṛhyamāṇakāraṇāḥ kiñcidantareṇa kasyāścidvidyāyāḥ pāraṅgatāḥ tatrabhavantaśśiṣṭāḥ* । — *Mahābhāṣyam*, 6-3-109

are *kumbhīdhānyāḥ*, i.e. they store cereals that are required for a short period (three days or so — see *Nyāyakandalī*, p. 670, *Praśastapādabhāṣyam*, Saṁpūrṇānanda, 1997), non-hoarders, non-greedy, follow the sacred path without reason (by nature), more or less have scholarship in all the branches of knowledge (got without teaching, exercise, etc.) through *tapas* and hence are venerated as *śiṣṭas*. As was already discussed in the first chapter of *Mahābhāṣya*, while it is possible to carry on the day-to-day transactions with either perfect *śabdas* or imperfect *śabdas*, one should prefer *sādhu* (perfect) *śabdas* (or *śabdas*) for the attainment of *dharma*, through the use of language. Abuse of language leads to *adharma*. Thus use and abuse of language are the subject matter of Vyākaraṇa, a system. Patañjali also clarifies that *śiṣṭa*'s language is authoritative and *Aṣṭādhyāyī* is useful in identifying *śiṣṭas*.

On the other hand, from the point of view of the mundane benefit, the use of *śabdas* is for transformation of meaning in an unambiguous and unequivocal manner. And since Vyākaraṇa has got usage as its base, there should be some standard language to prepare a standard Vyākaraṇa. That is what the trio, viz. Pāṇini, Kātyāyana and Patañjali strived for. Defects cannot be defined — declares Patañjali (Pā. 4-1-1). For that matter presently the linguists are trying hard for standardization of languages.

So far as the modern linguistics is concerned there are a few examples to show the concern of people about purism of language. A twelfth-century French poet, Garnier de Point — Sainte Maxence, assures his readers — "my way of speaking is good, for I was born in the Ile-de-France."

Relation of Śabda and Artha

Vaiyākaraṇas and Mīmāṁsakas believe that the relation between *śabda* and *artha* is eternal. Bhartṛhari[2] explains that the *śabda* has the natural capacity to express *artha* since time immemorial and this can be compared with sense-organs, i.e. eye, ear, etc. having the capacity (since time immemorial) to look, hear, etc. Naiyāyikas hold that *Īśvarecchā* (God's desire) is the cause of *śakti.*

On the Occidental side Plato (427-347 BCE) reached the conclusion that the meanings of words were determined by nature. Scholars from Aristotle onwards believed that meaning is determined by convention (*vṛddhavyavahāra*?).

However, it may be noted that generally *loka,* i.e. *vṛddhavyavahāra* (the usage of elders) is the way to know the meaning of a particular *śabda.*

Categorization of Śabdas

Earlier to Pāṇini (Śākaṭāyana and Nairuktas) there was fourfold division of *śabdas* — *nāma* (noun), *ākhyāta* (verb), *upasarga* (prefix) and *nipāta* (filler). Pāṇini preferred twofold division — *subanta* (noun) and *tiṅanta* (verb).

The three major form classes of Greek language were reflected from Aristotle onwards as three categories of prediction, viz. things (or substances), qualities, and actions. The one referred to by a noun is a thing, that referred by a verb is action and referents of adjectives are qualities.

---

2. *indriyāṇāṁ svaviṣayeṣvanādiryogyatā yathā* ।
anādirarthaiḥ śabdānāṁ sambandho yogyatā tathā ॥
— *Vākyapadīyam,* Pada-Sambandha - 29

Glossary

Abhidhā-vṛtti	Primary capacity of a word
Akhaṇḍa-vākya	The partless/indivisible sentence
Alaṁkāra	Figure of speech
Aluk	Non-disappearance (of a letter)
Anukaraṇa	Imitation
Anumāna	Inference
Anusaṁdhāna/upanaya	The connecting sentence
Anvaya	"If this (*varṇa*) is there this (meaning) will be there" (opp. *vyatireka*)
Arthavāda	Sentence of commendation or condemnation
Ādeśa	Replacement
Ākhyāta	Verb
Ātmā	Individual soul
Aucitya	Propriety
Aupaniṣadas	Followers of Upaniṣadic thought
Bhāṣā	Language. In *Pāṇinisūtras* it is spoken language opp. *chandas*/Veda
Dīrgha	Long vowel (*ā* — two *mātrās* of time)
Guṇa	Property, adjective, *guṇa-sandhi*
Ghanapāṭhī	a fifth level (*ghana*) Vedic scholar
Hetu/apadeśa	Reason

Hrasva	Short vowel (a — one *mātra* of time)
Iṭ	Cooked rice
Jāti/ākṛti/sāmānya	Class, DNA
Lakṣaṇā-vṛtti	Secondary capacity of a word
Lakṣyārtha	Secondary meaning
Lopa/Luk	Disappearance (of a letter)
Māyāvāda	A theory advocated by Śaṅkarācārya — "the world is myth and *Brahman* only is the truth"
Mokṣa	Salvation from worldly bindings, merging of individual soul with universal Soul
Nādānupradāna	The phoneme having *nāda* as an effort
Naiyāyikas	Logicians
Nipāta	Readymade word pronounced by Pāṇini; a filler in Prātiśākhyā
Nitya	Eternal; immutable
Nyāya	Logic; norm
Pañcama-svara	One of the seven notes — Cuckoo's call
Paramātmā/Brahman	Universal Soul; the cause of universe
Pātañjalayoga	The *Yogānuśāsana* compiled by Patañjali; Hiraṇyagarbha was the original author of Yoga
Pluta	Longer vowel (*a*3 — three *mātrā*s of time) used while calling a person at a distance; sun in Veda also
Prakriyā	Grammatical application
Pramāṇa	Means of Knowledge

Pratibhā	Capacity inherent or otherwise (ref. Vākyakāṇḍa of *Vākyapadīya*)
Pratijñā	A proposition
Pratyakṣa	Perception
Pratyāmnāya / nigamana	Conclusion
Prayoga	Usage
Puruṣārtha	The purpose of life (of a human being)
Śabda	Statement (Means of Knowledge)
Samit	Sacred stick
Saṁskāra	Refinement (untranslatable)
Saṁyoga	A cluster of letters; Association
Śāstram	Set of rules; rule, science
Śiṣṭas	Āryas
Śruti	Veda (learnt through hearing)
Sthāna	Place of utterance
Subanta	Noun
Sūtrakāra	Author of *sūtras*
Sūtram	Aphorism; Maxim; an elliptical sentence
Tanūnapāt	Fire
Tātparya	Purport; intention
Tattva	A basic thing/noumenon
Tat-tvam-asi	*Tat* = That, *Brahman*; *tvam* = You; *asi* = are
Tiṅanta/ākhyāta/kriyā	Verb
Udāharaṇa / nidarśana	Example
Upamāna	Simile

Upasarga	Prefix (ex. *pra, parā, ati*)
Upavedas	Āyurveda, Dhanurveda, Gāndharvaveda and Arthaśāstra
Vācyārtha	Primary meaning
Vāda	Argument
Vākyārtha	Sentence-meaning
Vāstu	Architecture
Vṛddhi	Increase, *vṛddhi-sandhi*
Vaiyākaraṇa	Grammarian, one who studies or knows Vyākaraṇa
Vyakti/dravyam	Individual
Vyaṅgyārtha/dhvani	Suggested meaning denoted by Vyañjanā
Vyañjanā-vṛtti	Suggestive capacity of a word
Vyatireka	"If this (*varṇa*) is not there that (meaning) will not be there" (opp. *anvaya*)
Vyavahāra	Usage
Yoga	Regulating/Controlling the mind

Bibliography

Oriental

Agniveśa, *Caraka Saṁhitā*, Part II, Siddhisthānam, Varanasi: Chowkhamba, 1983.

Akṣapāda, *Nyāyasūtram, Nyāyabhāṣyam*, Varanasi: Chowkhamba, 1925.

Ānandavardhana, *Dhvanyāloka*, Delhi: Motilal Banarsidass, 1963.

Annambhaṭṭa, *Tarkasaṁgraha*, Madras: Vavilla Press, 1960.

Atharvaveda, New Delhi: Nag Prakashan, 1986.

Bhartṛhari, *Vākyapadīyam*, Poona: Bhandarkar, 1978.

Bhaṭṭojidīkṣita, *Vaiyākaraṇasiddhāntakaumudī*, Mylapore, Madras: Balamanorama Press, 1929.

———, *Prauḍhamanoramā*, Varanasi: Chowkhamba, 1934.

———, *Śabdakaustubha*, Varanasi: Chowkhamba, 1929.

Bhoja, *Śṛṅgāraprakāśa*, Mysore: Srinivasa Josyar, 1963.

Gadādharabhaṭṭa, *Gādādharī*, Varanasi: Chowkhamba, 1970.

Jagadīśa, *Śabdaśaktiprakāśikā*, Varanasi: Chowkhamba, 1973.

Jagannāthapaṇḍitarāja, *Rasagaṅgādhara*, Sampūrṇānanda, Varanasi, 1996.

Jaimini, *Pūrvamīmāṁsādarśanam*, Poona: Anandasram, 1930.

Kaiyaṭa, *Mahābhāṣyapradīpa*, Varanasi: Chowkhamba, 1986.

Kālidāsa, *Raghuvaṁśa*, Varanasi: Chowkhamba, 1996.

Kaṇāda, *Vaiśeṣikadarśanam*, Varanasi: Chowkhamba, 1926.

Kātyāyana, *Vājasaneyaprātiśākhya*, ed. V.V. Sharma, Madras, 1934.

———, *Vārttikas, Mahābhāṣyam*, Varanasi: Chowkhamba, 1981.

Kauṇḍabhaṭṭa, *Bhuṣaṇasāra*, Delhi: Chowkhamba, 1989.

Kauṭilya, *Arthaśāstram*, Delhi: Bharatiya Vidya Prakashan, 1990.

Kumārilabhaṭṭa, *Ślokavārtikam*, Poona: Anandasram, 1930.

———, *Tantravārtikam*, Poona: Anandasram, 1930.

———, *Tupṭīkā*, Poona: Anandasram, 1930.

Mammaṭācārya, *Kāvyaprakāśa*, Jaikrishnadas, Benaras, 1926.

Nāgeśabhaṭṭa, *Vaiyākaraṇasiddhāntalaghumañjūṣā*, Varanasi: Chowkhamba, 1973.

———, *Mahābhāṣyapradīpa, Mahābhāṣya*, Varanasi: Chowkhamba, 1973.

———, *Laghuśabdenduśekhara*, Varanasi: Chowkhamba, 1926.

———, *Paribhāṣenduśekhara*, Visakhapatnam: Andhra University, 1973.

———, *Sphoṭavāda*, Madras: Adyar Library, 1930.

Pāṇini, *Aṣṭādhyāyī, Mahābhāṣyam*, Varanasi: Chowkhamba, 1986.

Patañjali, *Mahābhāṣyam*, Varanasi: Chowkhamba, 1986.

Prabhākara, *Bṛhati*, Nirṇayasagar, Mumbai, 1931.

Praśastapāda, *Praśaśtapādabhāṣyam*, Varanasi: Chowkhamba, 1926, Sampūrṇānanda, 1997.

Rāmānujācārya, *Śrībhāṣyam*, Vedāntadeśikavihārasabhā, 1960.

Ṛgvedaprātiśākhya, Kāśī Hindūviśvavidyālaya, 1970.

Ṛgveda, New Delhi: Nag Prakashan, 1996.

Śabarasvāmī, *Śābarabhāṣyam*, Poona: Anandasram, 1930.

Śākaṭāyana, *Ṛkprātiśākhya*, ed. & tr. M.D. Shastri, Allahabad, 1931.

Sāṁkhyasūtrāṇi, Varanasi: Ratna Publications, 1996.

Śaṅkarācārya, *Śāṅkarabhāṣyam on Brahmasūtras*, Panduranga Jawaji, Bombay, 1938.

Sāyaṇamādhava, *Sarvadarśanasaṁgraha*, Poona: Bhandarkar Oriental, 1978.

Subrahmanyam, Korada, *Mahāvākyavicāraḥ*, 1986.

———, *Vākyapadīyam*, Brahmakāṇḍa (English tr.), New Delhi: Sri Sadguru Publications, 1992.

———, *Four Vṛttis in Pāṇini*, 2001.

Śikṣāsaṁgraha, ed. Ramaprasada Tripathi, Varanasi: Sampurnanda Sanskrit University, 1989.

Suśruta, *Suśruta Saṁhitā*, Part II, Uttaratantram Adhyāya 65, Varanasi: Chowkhamba, 1990.

Udayanācārya, *Nyāyavārttikatātparyapariśuddhiḥ*, Varanasi: Chowkhamba.

Vālmīki, *Śrīmadvālmīkirāmāyaṇam*, Varanasi: Chowkhamba, 1996.

Viśvanātha, *Sāhityadarpaṇam*, New Delhi: Motilal Banarsidass, 1970.

Vyāsa, *Śrīmadbhāgavatam*, Varanasi: Chowkhamba, 1996.

Yajurveda, New Delhi: Nag Prakashan, 1996.

Yāska, *Niruktam*, Maheschandra Lakshmandas, 1963.

Occidental

Beatriz, R. Lavandera, *Linguistics : The Cambridge Survey*, ed. Fredric K. J. Newmeyer, vol. IV, Cambridge University Press, 1988.

Beaugrande, Robert-Alainde and Wolfgang Ulrich Dressler, *Introduction to Text Linguistics*, German ed. by Max Niemeyer Verlag Tübingan, 1972, English Translation, Logman, London & New York, 1981.

Blakemore, *The Ogranization of Discourse in Linguistics : The Cambridge Survey*, ed. Fredric K.J. Newmeyer, vol. IV, Cambridge University Press, 1988.

Bloomfield, Leonard, *Language*, Holt, New York: Rinehart and Winston, 1933.

Carnap, Rudolf (1939), *Foundations of Logic and Mathematics*, Foundations of Unity of Science : Towards an International Encyclopaedia of Unified Science, ed. Otto Neurath, Rudolf Carnap and Charles Morris, Chicago: University of Chicago Press, 1955.

Chomsky, Noam, *Syntactic Structures*, Mouton, The Hague, 1957.

———, *A Transformational Approach to Syntax*, Third Texas Conference on Problems of Linguistic Analysis of English, University of Texas, Austin, 1958.

———, *Aspects of the Theory of Syntax*, Cambridge: MIT Press, Mass, 1965.

———, *Topics of the theory of Generative Grammar*, The Hague, Mouton.

Li, Charles N. (ed.), *Subject and Topic*, Academic Inc., New York, 1976.

Christoperson, P. & A.O. Sandved, *An Advanced English Grammar*, Macmillan, 1969.

Corder, P. S., *Introducing Applied Linguistics*, Penguin Education, 1973.

Cowan, W. & J. Pakusan, *Source Book for Linguistics*, Benjamin Paperbacks, 1985.

Crystal, D., *Linguistics*, Penguin, 1971.

Elson, B. & V. Rickett, *An Introduction to Morphology & Syntax*, Summer Institute of Linguistics, Santana, California, 1969.

Figurovskij, I.A., *Sintaksis Celogo Teksta Uceniceskia Pis' mennye raboty* (Syntax of a whole text and pupils written work) Moscow, 1961, Linguistics, An International Review, 131, Mouton, 1974.

Freedle Roy, O. (ed.), *Discourse Production and Comprehension*, vol. I, New York: Ablex Publishing Corporation, Norwood, 1977.

Gipper, Helmut, *Studies in Western Linguistics*.

Gleason Jr., A.H., *An Introduction to Descriptive Linguistics*, Calcutta: Oxford & IBH Publishing Company, 1966.

Haegeman, Liliane, *Introduction to Government & Binding Theory*, Oxford: Blackwell, 1993.

Hall, Robert A., *Introductory Linguistics*, Delhi: Motilal Banarsidass, 1969.

Halliday, M.A.K., *The Linguistic Science & Language Teaching*, London: ELBS, 1975.

Handout, A., *Minimal Framework for Analysing Cohesion*, M.A. (Linguistics) Madras University, Madras, 1988.

Harris, Zellig, *Discourse Analysis*, Language, vol. 28.

———, *Methods of Structural Linguistics*, Chicago: University of Chicago Press, 1951.

———, *Transfer Grammar*, International Journal of American Linguistics, 1954 A.

———, *Papers in Structural and Transformational Linguistics*, 1954 B.

Hatim B. & I. Mason, *Discourse and the Translator*, Longman, Inc. New York 1990.

Hill, A.A., *Linguistics Today*, New York: Basic Books, 1969.

Hocket, Charles F., *A Course in Modern Linguistics*, New York: Macmillan, 1958.

Humboldt, Wilhelm von, *On Language* (tr. Peter Heath) Cambridge: Cambridge University Press, 1988.

Jesperson, O., *The Philosophy of Grammar*, London, 1924.

Jones, Linder Kay, *Theme in English Expositery Discourse*, Lake Bluff, Illinois: Jupiter Press, 1977.

Joseph & Grimes, *The Thread of Discourse*, Mouton, The Hague, 1975.

Journal of Comparative Philosophy, 1921.

Journal of the Linguistic Society of America, 1925.

Kasyap, Mankada, *Deixis and Discourse Structure*, 56th A/C of Linguistics, New Delhi: JNU, 1974.

Koerner, E.F.K., ed., *Amsterdam Studies in the Theroy & History of Linguistic Science IV, Current Issues in Linguistic Theory*, vol. I, Amsterdam, John Benjamins BV, 1975.

Leemberg, E.H., *Biological Foundations of Language*, Wiley, 1967.

Li, Charles N. (ed.), *Subject and Topic*, Academic Inc., New York, 1976.

Linguistics, An International Review, Mouton, 1974.

Lyons, J., *Introduction to Theoretical Linguistics*, Cambridge, 1971.

Marrifield, Willium, R. et al., *Morphology, Syntax, Laboratory Manual*, Summer Institute of Linguistics, California: Glendale, 1960.

Melmikov, G.P., Sistemnya Linguisticka, I. Iyo Otnosheniya K. Strukstoornon (in Russian) *In Problemi Izi Koznniya*, Moscow.

Newmeyer, Fredrick J. (ed.), *Linguistic Theory in America*, 2nd edn., Academic Press Inc., Orlando, 1986.

Nida, Eugene A., *Componental Analysis of Meaning: An Introducation to Semantic Structures*, Mouton: The Hague, 1975.

———, *Morphology: A Descriptive Analysis of Words*, 1049, University of Michigan Press, 1949.

Palmer, F., *Grammar*, ELBS, 1971.

Parret, *Connaissance Et Contextualite*, Amsterdam: Benjamins, 1980.

Pieter, A.M. Seuren, *Discourse Semantics*, Basil Blackwell, 1985.

Pike, Kenneth Lee, *Phonetics : A Critical Analysis of Phonetic Theory and a Technic for the Practical Description of Sounds*, Ann Arbor, Michigan, University of Michigan Press, 1943.

———, *Linguistic Concepts: An Introduction to Tagmemics*, London: University of Nebraska Press, 1982.

———, *Phonetics: A Technique for Reducing Languages to Writing*, Ann Arbor, Michigan, University of Michigan Press, 1947.

Rognar, Rommetveit, *Words, Meanings and Messages*, New York: Academic Press, 1968.

Thomson, A. J. and Martinet A.V., *A Practical English Grammar*, Oxford University Press, 1969.

Trait, Ronald L., *Patterns in Clause, Sentence and Discourse*, Publication of Summer Institute of Linguistics of the University of Oklahama, Norman, 1973.

Trait, Ronald, L. et al., *Patterns in Clause: A Sentence & Discourse in Selected Languages of India & Nepal*, 1973.

Trudgill, Pater, *Sociolinguistics: An Introduction.*

Index